D0474742

Kneeling We Triumph

By the same Authors:

The Christian's Daily Challenge
King's Diamond
Royal Exchange
Royal Counsel
Royal Purpose
Soul Sculpture

Kneeling
We Triumph

Compiled by
Edwin and Lillian Harvey

M.O.V.E. PRESS
1 St. Thomas Terrace, Blackburn, Lancs.

Cover and typographic designs
by James S. Taylor, A.R.C.A.

Cover design based on a 16th Century memorial
brass at Cookham Parish Church.

Printed in England
by Peter Scott Ltd., Burnley, Lancs.

Acknowledgments

In seeking to obtain permission to use copyright material we have met with a most courteous and kindly response from both publishers and authors. We take this occasion to express our thanks in the following instances: The Allahabad Bible Seminary (O.M.S.) for the selection by Dr. Wesley Duewel from "Revival" magazine; Mr. George E. Failing for quotations by Dr. Oliver G. Wilson and poems by Edith Bang, Mrs. Nina Hard Crosby and Barbara Cornet Ryberg from "The Wesleyan Methodist"; God's Revivalist Press for quotations by G. D. Watson and Martin Wells Knapp; The Editor, "The Alliance Witness", for exerpts by Dr. A. W. Tozer and Dr. A. B. Simpson; Rev. Armin R. Gesswein for quotations from his own writings; Mrs. C. E. C. Gladwell for the poem by Charles B. Bowser from the periodical, "The Message of God"; The Editor, "Herald of Holiness", for the poems by F. W. David, John W. Little and Jessie Whiteside Finks; Mrs. V. Hood for the poem, "Go, Wait Before Him", by Edith Hickman Divall; Messrs. Hodder & Stoughton Ltd. for the selections by Samuel Chadwick, Sister Eva of Friedenshort, G. Campbell Morgan and J. R. Mott; Macmillan of London and Basingstoke for the selection by Sadhu Sundar Singh from the book, "The Sadhu", by Streeter and Appasamy; Marshall, Morgan & Scott Ltd. for quotations by Gordon B. Watt from his book, "Effectual Fervent Prayer"; Overseas Missionary Fellowship for selections by J. O. Fraser, D. E. Hoste, Hudson Taylor, Mrs. Howard Taylor and Pastor Hsi; The Paternoster Press for the quotations by G. H. Lang; Mr. Leonard Ravenhill for extracts from his book, "Why Revival Tarries"; Dr. Alan Redpath for the extract from

his writings; Fleming H. Revell Company for the quotations by
S. D. Gordon from his book, "Quiet Talks on Prayer";
S.P.C.K. for the selections by Lilias Trotter from the book,
"The Master of The Impossible", edited by Constance E.
Padwick, the quotation by Amy Wilson Carmichael from her
biography, "Amy Carmichael of Dohnavur", by Frank Houghton,
and the extract by Thomas Walker from "Walker of Tinnevelly"
by Amy Wilson Carmichael; The Sunday School Times
Federation for the selection by Dr. Charles G. Trumbull;
Worldwide Evangelistic Crusade for the extract by C. T. Studd
from "The Laugh of Faith".

Many of the poems, quotations and extracts used in the book
have been gleaned over a period of years from such varied
sources that in numbers of cases it has been impossible, after
considerable effort, to trace either the publisher or the author.
Where omissions have been made and due credit has not been
given, we beg indulgence.

Foreword

Like many other Christian workers who have been anxious to be successful in labour for God we have been forced to the conclusion that the Holy Spirit alone can effect lasting results. During these past years of heart-searching study, we have gathered together similar conclusions from many God-honoured ministers and missionaries who have discovered the secret that the Holy Spirit comes to our aid when, wearied with self-effort, we ask, seek and knock. We long very much to share with God's children some of these readings and to spread them as widely as possible. We ask humbly that the lives and labours of many who read will be revived and blessed by the pages of "Kneeling We Triumph" in Books I and II.

Each book contains sixty readings which are a storehouse of precious nuggets on the subject that we have arranged in what seems to us logical divisions such as "Importance of Prayer", "Time for Prayer", "Prayer and Communion", "Hindrances to Prayer", "Persevering Prayer", "Intercessory Prayer" and "Prayer and Faith".

We express our indebtedness to our many friends and prayer partners who have so encouraged us in this work. We especially thank our fellow-workers who have so unstintingly aided in proof-reading, typing and in many other ways. We now send forth "Kneeling We Triumph" with the earnest prayer that the message will help toward a reviving of prayer on all fronts.

Edwin and Lillian Harvey.

Prayer
releases God's power

And whatsoever ye shall ask in my name, that will I do, that the Father may be glorified in the Son. If ye shall ask anything in my name, I will do it. John 14 : 13, 14.

Call unto me and I will answer thee, and shew thee great and mighty things, which thou knowest not. Jer. 33 : 3.

Prayer does not release some mere force of man or nature. Prayer releases the immeasurable wealth and power of Almighty God! "Call unto Me, and I will answer thee, and shew thee great and mighty things, which thou knowest not." Jer. 33 : 3. There you have it. "I will shew thee great and mighty things." It is the voice of God!

It is the omnipotent Sovereign Creator and Sustainer of a hundred million universes, as astronomers are wont to speak of creation today, Who here gives us His Word!

He says, in effect, that if you will pray, He will work! He, with Whom nothing is impossible, Who spoke—and worlds without number came into being, pledges His most holy and immutable Word that, if we will but seek His face in prayer— He will work, and bring to pass great and mighty things such as have never been entertained in the mind and thought of man. (Read John 14 : 12-14).

It is when men bow the knee and call upon God that, in a sense, they become as mighty as the Almighty. Do not misunderstand me. I am not being irreverent. I am only saying what He says in His Holy Word, "Call unto Me, and I will answer thee, and shew thee great and mighty things, which thou knowest not." You pray, says the Almighty God, and I will work! If you ask anything in My name, I will do it. "And call upon Me in the day of trouble : I will deliver thee, and thou shalt glorify Me." Psa. 50 : 15. **F. J. Huegel.**

There is no wonder more supernatural and divine in the life of the believer than the mystery and the ministry of prayer . . .

wonder of wonders! Mystery of mysteries! Miracle of miracles! The hand of the child touching the arm of the Father and moving the wheels of the universe. Beloved, this is your supernatural place and mine, and over its gates we read the inspiring invitation. "Thus saith Jehovah, call unto me and I will answer thee, and shew thee great and mighty things, which thou knowest not." **Dr. A. B. Simpson.**

This promise, given to Jeremiah, was Dr. Simpson's great life text, and became the foundation of that daring faith which was the secret of his mighty ministry. It led him to exhort us to "see that our highest ministry and power is to deal with God for men" and to believe that "our highest form of service is the ministry of prayer."

Dr. Simpson had solved the secret of service when he learned the mystery of prayer. In prayer he received a vision of God's will. Through further prayer he ascertained God's plans for the carrying out of His will. Still praying, he was empowered to execute those plans. More prayer brought the supply of need for the work. Continuing still in prayer, he was able to carry through what he had begun. Praying always, a spirit of praise and adoration welled up in his heart, and God received all the glory for everything that was accomplished. **A. E. Thompson.**

> Some tell us that prayer is all in the mind,
> That the only result is the solace we find;
> That God does not answer, nor hear when we call:
> We commune with our own hearts in prayer;
>   that is all!
> But we who have knelt with our burden and care,
> And have made all our problems a matter of prayer,
> Have seen God reach down from His heaven above,
> Move mountains, touch hearts, in His infinite love;
> We know that God works in a wonderful way
> On behalf of His children who trust Him **and pray.**
>
> **Barbara Cornet Ryberg**

The loftiest employment

And in the morning, rising up a great while before day, he went out, and departed into a solitary place, and there prayed. Mark 1 : 35.

He was alone praying. Luke 9 : 18.

Then said Jesus, Father, forgive them; for they know not what they do. Luke 23 : 34.

Jesus Christ was essentially the Teacher of prayer by precept and example. We have glimpses of His praying which, like indices, tell how full of prayer the pages, chapters and volumes of His life were. The epitome which covers not one segment only but the whole circle of His life, and character, is pre-eminently that of prayer. The Suppliant of all suppliants He was, the Intercessor of all intercessors. In lowliest form He approached God, and with strongest pleas He prayed and supplicated. Jesus Christ, a man, the God-man, the highest illustration of manhood, is Mediator between God and man. Jesus Christ, the Divine Man, died for all men. His death is but a prayer for all men.

On earth, Jesus Christ knew no higher law, no holier business, no diviner life, than to plead for men. On earth He lived and prayed and died for men. In Heaven He knows no more royal estate, no higher theme, than to intercede for men. His life, His death and His exaltation all plead for men.

Is there any work, higher work for the disciple to do than His Lord did ? Is there any loftier employment, more

E. M. Bounds.

> How oft He sought the mountain top, and knelt
> upon its crest,
> To pray and lay His weary head, upon His father's
> breast.
> Before He called the twelve to Him, He prayed all
> night alone,

And when the day began to dawn, He chose them
for His own.
They saw Him lift up holy hands, and raise His
tear-stained eyes;
Again they saw Him on His knees, and with new
strength arise.
The awe of His appealing words grew greater day
by day,
Until they humbly said to Him, "Lord, teach us how
to pray !"

Great Commission Prayer League

The thought of Christ's intercession has taken on a new
preciousness these last days. I was reading of one to whom
God had given a wonderful gift of prayer . . . and the thought
came, "Oh, that we had someone among us able to pray like
that !" And then, almost with the vividness of an audible voice
came the further thought, "Is not Jesus enough ?" And the
sense of praying with Him, praying alongside, has been
beautiful these days. **Lilias Trotter.**

S. D. Gordon says of Christ's intercession : "The Lord Jesus is
still praying. Thirty years of living; three years of serving; one
tremendous act of dying; nineteen hundred years of prayer.
What an emphasis on prayer !"
All the crises in the life of our Lord were linked with special
seasons of prayer, and His teaching set forth wonderful
assurances to those who pray. **Samuel Chadwick.**

He teaches us to pray not only by example, by instruction, by
command, by promises, but by showing us Himself, the
ever-living Intercessor, as our Life. It is when we believe this,
and go and abide in Him for our prayer life too, that our
fears of not being able to pray aright will vanish, and we shal
joyfully and triumphantly trust our Lord to teach us to pray, to
be Himself the life and the power of our prayer.
   May God open our eyes to see what the holy ministry of
intercession is to which, as His royal priesthood, we have
been set apart. May He give us a large and strong heart to
believe what mighty influence our prayers can exert. And may
all fear as to our being able to fulfil our vocation vanish as
we see Jesus, living ever to pray, living in us to pray, and
standing surety for our prayer life. **Andrew Murray.**

Unlimited possibilities

Unto him that is able to do exceeding abundantly above all that we ask or think, according to the power that worketh in us, unto him be glory . . . by Christ Jesus throughout all ages, world without end. Eph. 3 : 20, 21.

Prove me now . . . saith the Lord of hosts. Mal. 3 : 10.

"Above all we ask." The ability of God is beyond our prayers, beyond our largest prayers! I have been thinking of some of the petitions that have entered into my supplications innumerable times . . . Sometimes I have thought that my asking was too presumptuous, it was even beyond the power of God to give. And yet here comes the apostolic doxology: "above all we ask." What I have asked for is nothing compared to the ability of my God to give. I have asked for a cupful, and the ocean remains! I have asked for a sunbeam, and the sun abides! My best asking falls immeasurably short of my Father's giving. It is beyond all that we ask. **J. H. Jowett.**

There is a valley in Italy called Larderello Valley. It is called the Valley of Hell because it is a very ugly valley, sitting on top of a volcano. Here the white hot interior of the earth comes closer to the earth's surface than is normal elsewhere.

A Frenchman, Count de Larderello, noticed white deposits that were left in the little pools in the valley where the steam pushing its way through the earth's crust left deposits of water. He asked of these pools and they gave minerals.

But in 1904 more daring experiments were made and five electric bulbs were lit by power generated by the steam. A more intrepid man bored into the earth's surface, and steamy vapours hurtled themselves thousands of feet into the air. There was power unlimited, but the task was to harness and utilise this untapped form of energy. 13% of Italy's entire electricity needs were met as pipelines were laid conveying the power to the industrial and population centres. Doubtless much more may still be realised by those asking more from this unlimited source of power.

Five electric bulbs or endless energy. We limit God by our timid asking and failing to harness by prayer that immeasurable Almightiness of God. God has said His power was unlimited. "With God nothing shall be impossible unto you." He has told us to "ask" and promised that we should receive. The tragedy of most of our lives is what we miss. Trivialities absorb us while all the time God's almightiness is available !

May our prayer be like David's : "O God forsake me not; until I have shewed thy strength unto this generation, and thy power to every one that is to come." Psa. 71 : 18.

We doubt the word that tells us : Ask,
    And ye shall have your prayer;
We turn our thoughts as to a task,
    With will constrained and rare.

And yet we have; these scanty prayers
    Yield gold without alloy :
O God, but he that trusts and dares
    Must have a boundless joy !

G. MacDonald

The Word of God represents all the possibilities of God as at the disposal of true prayer. Help is at hand, and often comes before the prayer is yet complete, because He hears the unspoken sigh and groan. God's supplies are inexhaustible; His ability and willingness are both infinite; hence His answers often transcend all our requests or even imaginings. When the praying suppliant abides in Christ, as the branch in the vine, his supplications are but one form of the development and expression of the Life of Christ in him, just as the buds, blossoms and clusters of the branch are expressions of the vine's vitality. Prayer brings peace by banishing care, transferring burdens to the great Burden Bearer. **A. T. Pierson.**

Life bringing prayer

He is a prophet, and he shall pray for thee, and thou shalt live. Gen. 20 : 7.

So Abraham prayed unto God : and God healed Abimelech. Gen. 20 : 17.

He . . . shut the door upon them twain, and prayed unto the Lord. II Kings 4 : 33.

"Our strength has been often expended upon externals of our work; and we have failed to attain, in any adequate degree, the main aspect of our mission—that immortal souls might have life, and that they might have it more abundantly." These are the words of a missionary, Thomas Walker of Tinnevelly in South India, after years on the field. Asking an Indian pastor how many among his twenty to thirty congregations had life, the man replied that there were only two or three, but he could only be certain of one. Walker determined to displace other things and make way for the kind of prayer that would speak life into dead souls. He continues :

"A lad is lying in the prophet's chamber, still and motionless in the deep sleep of death. The servant of the man of God, in obedience to his master's bidding, runs in eager haste and lays the prophet's staff upon the face of the child, apparently expecting that the first contact of the rod would restore the dead to life again. The result is told in graphic language, pathetic in its simplicity and truth : 'There was neither voice, nor hearing.'

"Then came the man of God himself. But as he looked upon the scene before him, it was the still and awful scene of death. What will Elisha do ? His rod has wrought no miracle. His servant's rush of haste has done absolutely nothing. Notice well the words which follow : 'He went in therefore and shut the door upon them twain, and prayed unto the Lord.' What the eager haste could not do, what the touching with his rod was unable to effect, the power of prayer could bring to pass; and therefore he got him to that inner chamber and prayed unto the Lord. His prayer was fervent, believing, and full of yearning sympathy for that poor sleeper.

"We may well pause to ask whether we have not failed in getting into loving touch with those amongst whom we live and work. Let us lay stress upon the fact that the rush and the rod of office produced not the shadow of a real change, and only ended in the sad confession, 'The child is not awaked.' Fellow-workers, we may run about our work in one long rush of busy labour, we may take our wand of missionary office and place it in every zenana and wave it at every street corner; but if that is all we do, Satan will rejoice and we shall be ashamed before him.

"Do not many of us need first of all a personal awakening? We have got into a routine of work, and can show an honourable record at the close of every day of business accomplished, visits paid, classes taught, addresses given. But in the light of eternity are we satisfied with that? Have souls been really sought, yearned over, loved and won? Is ours fruit that will remain? We may even persuade hundreds, especially of the poorer classes, to accept baptism and enrol themselves as Christians; but are we sure that they are God's converts and not merely the manufactured article? Are we working ourselves with the Fire of God, and not merely using the artificial fire, the strange fire of our own fleshly energy?

"When Zechariah was aroused as a man, that is wakened out of his sleep, what did he see? He saw the golden candlestick with its pipes, through which the oil flowed from the olive trees; and he learnt in that vision the secret of spiritual power. 'Not by might, nor by power, but by my spirit, saith the Lord of hosts.' "

No blessing without asking

In everything by prayer and supplication let your requests be made known unto God. And the peace of God, which passeth all understanding, shall keep your hearts and minds through Christ Jesus. Phil. 4 : 6, 7.

Go in peace : and the God of Israel grant thee thy petition that thou hast asked of him. I Sam 1 : 17.

Whatsoever you desire or want, either for others, or for your own soul, "Ask, and it shall be given you."

The neglect of prayer is a grand hindrance to holiness. "We have not because we ask not." Oh, how meek and gentle, how lowly in heart, how full of love both to God and man, might you have been at this day, if you had only asked, if you had continued instant in prayer! ASK, that you may thoroughly experience and perfectly practise the whole of that religion which our Lord so beautifully described in the Sermon on the Mount. **John Wesley.**

God will not let me get the blessing without asking. Today I am setting my face to fast and pray for enlightenment and refreshing. Until I can get up to the measure of at least two hours in pure prayer every day, I shall not be contented. Meditation and reading besides. **Andrew Bonar.**

Prayer asks; faith expects. Some of God's gifts come without asking. Sun and rain bless the earth whether we pray or not. Life-sustaining atmosphere surrounds the earth apart from our prayers. God takes care of his earth like a good property owner cares for his home.

But none of God's best gifts come without asking. No-one is saved unless he prays—**"Whosoever shall call upon the name of the Lord shall be saved."** No-one receives the wisdom he needs apart from prayer—**"If any man lack wisdom, let him ask of God . . . and it shall be given him."** Joshua was not aware of the deceitfulness of the Gibeonites because **"he asked not** counsel at the mouth of the Lord!

Asking alone is not enough. **"Let him ask in faith, nothing wavering."** In other words, pray expectantly. God answers us when we talk to Him; He does not merely hear us. Sincere prayer, with faith, is always recognised and rewarded. **George Failing.**

In the diary of Dr. Chalmers, we find recorded this petition: "Make me sensible of real answers to actual requests, as evidences of an interchange between myself on earth and my Saviour in Heaven."

Prayer is the child's request, not to the winds nor to the world, but to the Father. Prayer is the outstretched arms of the child for Father's help. Prayer is the child's cry calling to the Father's ear, the Father's heart, and to the Father's ability, which the Father is to hear, the Father is to feel, and which the Father is to relieve. Prayer is the seeking of God's great and greatest good, which will not come if we do not pray.

Prayer is an ardent and believing cry to God for some specific thing. God's rule is to answer by giving the specific thing asked for. With it may come much of other gifts and graces. Strength, serenity, sweetness, and faith may come as the bearers of the gifts. But even they come because God hears and answers prayer. **E. M. Bounds.**

> When thoughts take wings
> And fly to God,
>   That's Prayer!
> When "Dominant Desire"
> Mounts on wordless wings—
>   That's really Prayer.
> When Love, Praise, and Thanksgiving
> Ascend in ecstacy—
>   That's exultant Prayer!
> When Faith takes hold upon
> God's promises and says,
>   "It shall be done,"
>   That is prevailing Prayer!

Mrs. Nina Hard Crosby

Prayer power

As a prince hast thou power with God and with men, and hast prevailed. Gen. 32:28.

The God of Israel is he that giveth strength and power unto his people. Psa. 68:35.

There is no greater power in the world than prayer. True prayer can do anything, the prayer that is wrought by the Spirit and is presented at the Throne of the omnipotent God in the Name of Christ. The greatest promises in the Bible concern prayer. Jesus Christ, the supreme Intercessor, gave to His followers the privilege of prayer, and none can tell the immensity of the sphere He opened to them (John 14:12-15).

He who has been allowed to tarry in the Presence of the Lord, carries a divine atmosphere with him into everyday life, the glory light illumines everything he touches. His heart is continually drawn to that inner sanctuary, and he counts the day drab and dreary in which he has not crossed the threshold into the holy place.

We find men of all stations and all ages, from thoughtful children to dying patriarchs, in this shining throng of praying souls who have carried the victorious banner of the Gospel through the world, and have wrought mighty works in prayer. Hard-pressed mothers, artisans, labourers, scholars, servant-girls, soldiers, dignitaries of the Church, poor ignorant laymen, little boys and girls, lonely widows, and sick folk on their beds of pain, they are all in the great army of God; they fight invisible battles and win victories. The secret of their lives is sometimes revealed here on earth, but in most cases it will be on the other side, when causes and results are unveiled in the Light of Glory, that we shall know them.

The source of true power lies in prayer. Prayer is the secret of success in the realm of the Spirit and of Love. Many a restless, defeated life would be transformed if it became a life of prayer. What costs nothing is worth nothing. Prayer does cost something. It costs much! He who would pray must deny himself, he must give his whole time and strength to the service of God. ***Sister Eva of Friedenshort.**

A day without prayer is a day without blessing, and a life without prayer is a life without power.

D. E. Hoste, successor to Hudson Taylor as Director of the China Inland Mission, stressed the need to find time to pray, and states: "It is a commonplace to say that prayer and secret devotion are important; too often, however, we virtually contradict the words by adding that it is impossible to find time for them. This simply means that, as a matter of fact, we do not regard them as of the first importance. As a rule, we allow at least an hour and a half in the day for the nourishment of our bodies. Why should we expect our Christian life to be strong and helpful to others if less time is given to secret devotions?"

> Prayer is a privilege that God has giv'n
> To mortal man. Of all the gifts of Heav'n
> Few are greater, and none we use the less.
> Prayer lifts the heavy burdens that would press
> Upon the soul; it heals the broken heart,
> And worries, cares, and troubles all depart.
> It calms the anxious, sets the mind at rest;
> And he who really prays is truly blest.
> Wherefore, O mortal man, lift up thy head,
> And pray, and seek the face of Him Who said,
> "Come unto me . . . and I will give you rest."
> Believe His Word and tell Him your request;
> Be not cast down, but go to God in prayer;
> He'll solve your problem, lift your every care.

Everek R. Storms

From The True Meaning of Life by Sister Eva Friedenshort. (London: Hodder & Stoughton). Copyright 1937 by China Inland Mission.

Jesus opens the way to prayer

Jesus saith . . . I am the way . . . No man cometh unto the Father but by me. John 14 : 6.

I am the door: by me if any man enter in, he shall be saved, and shall go in and out, and find pasture. John 10 : 9.

Immediately upon Adam's sin, the door of communion with God was locked, yea, chained up, and no more coming nigh the Lord : not a soul could have access to Him, either in a way of communion in this world, or of enjoyment in that to come. It was Jesus the Mediator that opened that door again, and in Him it is that we have boldness, and access with confidence. **Flavel.**

The basis of prayer is right relationship with God. The only basis of such relationship to God is Jesus. We have been outlawed by sin. Jesus came. He was God and man. We get back to God through Jesus, and only so.

The blood of the Cross is the basis of all prayer. Through it the relationship is established that underlies all prayer. Only as I come to God through Jesus—the blood of Jesus cleanseth from all sin—and only as I keep in sympathy with Jesus in the purpose of my life can I pray effectively.

Let us distinctly understand that we have no standing with God except through Jesus. **S. D. Gordon.**

Andrew Murray gives some very helpful advice to those who feel they are guilty of prayerlessness and want to learn to pray. "Many a one has turned to his Inner Chamber, under bitter self-accusation that he has prayed so little, and has resolved for the future to live in a different manner. Yet no blessing has come—there was not the strength to continue faithful because his eyes had not been fixed on the Lord Jesus. If he had only understood, he would have said : 'Lord, Thou seest how cold and dark my heart is : I know that I must pray, but feel I cannot do so; I lack the urgency and desire to pray.'

"He did not know that at that moment the Lord Jesus in His tender love was looking down upon him and saying: 'You cannot pray: you feel that all is cold and dark: why not give yourself over into My hands? Only believe that I am ready to help you in prayer; I long greatly to shed abroad My love in your heart, so that you, in the consciousness of weakness, may confidently rely on Me to bestow the grace of prayer. Just as I will cleanse you from all other sins, so also will I deliver from the sin of prayerlessness—only do not seek the victory in your own strength. Bow before Me as one who expects everything from his Saviour. Be assured of this—I will teach you how to pray.'

"Many a one will acknowledge: 'I see my mistake: I had not thought that the Lord Jesus must deliver and cleanse me from this sin also. I had not supposed that just as He will give all other grace in answer to prayer, so, above all and before all, He will bestow the grace of a praying heart. What folly to think that all other blessings must come from Him but that prayer, whereon everything else depends, must be obtained by personal effort! Thank God I begin to comprehend—the Lord Jesus is Himself in the Inner Chamber watching over me, and holding Himself responsible to teach me how to approach the Father . . .'

"I must believe in His infinite love, which really longs to have communion with me every moment and to keep me in the enjoyment of His fellowship. I must believe in His Divine power, which has conquered sin, and will truly keep me from it. I must believe in Him Who, as the great Intercessor, through the Spirit, will inspire each member of His Body with joy and power for communion with God in prayer. My prayer-life must be brought entirely under the control of Christ and His love."

> Thou art the Way!
>   All ways are thorny mazes without Thee;
> Where hearts are pierced, and thoughts all aimless
>   stray,
>   In Thee the heart stands firm, the life moves free:
> Thou art our Way!

By whom also we have access by faith. **Rom. 5 : 2.**

Prayer fulfils
the will of God

And this is the confidence that we have in him, that, if we ask any thing according to his will, he heareth us. I John 5 : 14.

For it is God which worketh in you both to will and to do of his good pleasure. Phil. 2 : 13.

Do we consult the Heavenly Government at the outset, or do we pray "the first thing that comes"? Do we spend much time waiting upon God to know His will, before attempting to embark on His promises? That this is a principle upon which God works He has informed us very plainly in I John 5 : 14. I cannot but feel that this is a cause (not the only cause) of many unanswered prayers. James 4 : 3 has a broad application, and we need to search our hearts in its light. **J. O. Fraser.**

"Does prayer change the will of God?" asks a Christian. It seems a knotty question. No. Actually, it is only by prayer, and in answer to prayer, that God's will is done on earth as it is in Heaven. This is another way of saying that so often— because we do not pray—the will of man, or of the flesh, or of Satan, is being done. That is just the trouble, and the crux of the matter.

This is just where the Bible comes in. A chaplain was kneeling in prayer with a group, as one by one they prayed, "Lord, if it be thy will . . ." He suggested that they all rise from their knees, take their Bibles, and find out what God's will was; and then go to prayer, praying that His will, revealed in His Word, be done.

This is the point where we must watch closely. The point of **reason** is that prayer changes God's will; the point of Scripture is that prayer realises God's will as revealed in God's Word.

Reason can also argue very subtly in the opposite direction: "God is sovereign. He is God, you know, and He will do this thing whether we pray about it or not." Nothing is closer to reason, at times, than this; yet, nothing is further from Scripture. For God will not do apart from prayer what He has promised to do in answer to prayer and it is my Christian responsibility to search the Scriptures and find out just what that is.

It has well been said, "When God is about to do a work, He always starts by getting His people to pray." It is only as we pray that we get what God can do.

Nothing lies outside the circle of prayer except what lies outside the orbit of God's will. **Armin Gesswein.**

And shall I pray Thee change Thy will, my Father,
   Until it be according unto mine?
But no, Lord, no, that never shall be, rather
   I pray Thee blend my human will with Thine.

I pray Thee hush the hurrying, eager longing
   I pray Thee soothe the pangs of keen desire.
See in my quiet places wishes thronging,
   Forbid them, Lord, purge, though it be with fire.

                                        Amy Carmichael

The carnal and worldly spirit cannot triumph in prayer, for carnality prompts to ask for gratification's sake, and would make prayer only another avenue of selfishness. Worldliness allies the soul with the world—the enemy of God. All worldly alliance is spiritual adultery. And how can the disciples who are coquetting with the very world that seeks to supplant the Divine Bridegroom in their affection and allegiance, go with acceptance to the very Lord whom these compromises dishonour to ask a favour! **A. T. Pierson.**

There is nothing more appalling than the wholesale way in which unthinking people plead to the Almighty the richest and most spiritual of His promises, and claim their immediate fulfilment, without themselves fulfilling one of the conditions either on which they are promised or can possibly be given. **H. Drummond.**

Watch your motives

When thou prayest, thou shalt not be as the hypocrites are:
for they love to pray . . . that they may be seen of men.
Matt. 6 : 5.

They think that they shall be heard for their much speaking.
Matt. 6 : 7.

Our Lord begins His teaching about prayer with a little playful
irony in which He tells the disciples to watch their motives
(Matt. 6 : 5). "Why do you want to pray? Do you want to be
known as a praying man? Well, verily that is your reward, you
will be known as a praying man, but there is no answer to
your prayer." The next thing He told them was to keep a
secret relationship between themselves and God (Matt. 6 : 6),
and in verse 7 He told them not to rely on their own
earnestness when praying. These three statements of Jesus,
which are so familiar to us, are revolutionary. Call a halt one
moment and ask yourself, "Why do I want to pray, what is my
motive? Have I a personal, secret relationship to God that
nobody knows but myself? And what is my method when I
pray, am I really relying on God or on my own earnestness?"

These sayings of Jesus go to the very root of all praying.
The majority of us make the blunder of depending on our own
earnestness and not on God at all. It is confidence in Him
that tells (I John 5 : 14, 15). All our fuss, all our earnestness,
all our "gifts of prayer" are not the slightest atom of use to
Jesus Christ, He pays no attention to them. Our Lord gave His
disciples the pattern prayer, and supplied in that prayer their
want of ideas and words and faith.

Then He taught them the prayer of patience. Our Lord's
instruction about patience in prayer conveys this lesson:
"If you are right with God, and God delays the manifested
answer to your prayer, don't misjudge Him, don't think of Him
as an unkind friend, or an unnatural father, or an unjust judge,
but keep at it. Your prayer will certainly be answered," says

Jesus, "for everyone that asks receives," and "men ought always to pray and not faint." Your Heavenly Father will explain it all one day, He cannot just now because He is developing your character. **Oswald Chambers.**

In my childhood I cried for all things; in manhood I dare not. I can still pray without ceasing, but I can no longer pray without limit. What if I ask the gold that was meant for another! What if I seek the place that was made for another! What if I claim the work that was planned for another! Methinks the pauses of prayer are more noble than its flights. In these pauses I say, "Not my will, but Thine." Are they not to Thee the finest parts of the music, O my Father! There is no architecture so beautiful to Thee as my arrested tower—my tower arrested that another may have room. Never let me build, even in my prayers, a house with so many mansions for myself that I cannot say to my brother, "I have prepared a place for you"! **G. Matheson.**

I asked of God that He should give success
To the high task I sought for Him to do;
I asked that every hindrance might grow less
And that my hours of weakness might be few;
I asked that far and lofty heights be scaled—
And now I humbly thank Him that I failed.

For with the pain and sorrow came to me
A dower of tenderness in act and thought;
And with the failure came a sympathy,
An insight which success had never brought.
Father, I had been foolish and unblest
If Thou hadst granted me my blind request.

Unknown

Men's obstinacy
not God's reluctance

If I regard iniquity in my heart, the Lord will not hear me.
Psa. 66 : 18.

If our heart condemn us, God is greater than our heart, and
knoweth all things. Beloved, if our heart condemn us not, then
have we confidence toward God. And whatsoever we ask, we
receive of him, because we keep his commandments, and do
those things that are pleasing in his sight. I John 3 : 20-22.

"If I regard iniquity in my heart, the Lord will not hear me."
What strikes us in the condition which David describes is its
deliberateness. It is not something into which a man may fall,
out of weakness, and almost without knowing it. To "regard
iniquity" is a voluntary act . . . The man or woman chooses
the sin, and chooses to cling to it. The deliberateness may
cloak itself and try to pass for a necessity. You may lay the
blame on circumstance, on temperament, on education, on
almost anything; but all the time down at the bottom of your
heart, in the moment when you are sincerely honest, you know
which are the sins you choose, which are the sins to which
you open the gate. You can tell them by a certain confidence
in their step as they enter and walk through the streets of
your heart. They are different from those that have climbed
in over the unguarded wall.

Do you not know what I am trying to describe so feebly?
Have you never felt sure that sin was harming you not merely
by what it made you **do,** but by what it made you **lose**?
There was a life with God, of which men told, of which
something in your own heart assured you of the possibility and
the beauty, from which you knew you were shut out, not
because of any unwillingness of God, but simply because of
the life you were living.

Years and years ago the whole story was told by Jesus in
the parable of the Prodigal Son. He never was turned out of his
father's house. A thousand slips and faults of his boyhood did
not separate him from his father so long as his **heart** was true
and loyal. Only when he rebelled and went away, his father

could not follow him, except with love. Only as long as he stayed away, his father, however much he loved him, could not be with him. But the moment he returned, the house was opened, the feast was spread, the communion was re-established. "While he was yet a great way off, his father saw him." There is no more to tell than that. A thousand sermons could tell no more. God **will** hear as soon as He **can** hear. It is man's obstinacy, not God's reluctance, that keeps back the mercy. **P. Brooks.**

Oswald Smith likewise affirms the same truth: "If we are to engage in this, the highest form of Christian service, we must be standing on praying ground. 'If I regard iniquity in my heart,' declares the inspired Word, 'the Lord will not hear me.' To be standing on praying ground is to have put away every sin, to turn from anything that grieves the Holy Spirit."

Dr. A. B. Simpson writes: "We cannot trust God in the face of wilful sin. An unsanctified state is fatal to any high degree of faith, for the carnal heart is not the soil in which it can grow. Faith is the fruit of the Spirit and is hindered by the weeds of sin and wilful indulgence. The reason many Christians have so little faith is because they are living in the world and in themselves, and separated in so large a part of their life from God and holiness. Faith requires for its heavenly vision the highlands of holiness and separation, and the clear blue sky of a consecrated life. Beloved, may you not find in this the explanation of many of your doubts and fears. Your plane is too low, your heart is too mixed, and your life is too near this 'present evil world.' "

Repudiate pretence in prayer

The true worshippers shall worship the Father in spirit and in truth: for the Father seeketh such to worship him. John 4:23.

Let us not love in word, neither in tongue; but in deed and in truth. I John 3:18.

A spiritual writer of unusual penetration has advised frankness in prayer even to a degree that might appear to be downright rudeness. When you come to prayer, he says, and find that you have no taste for it, tell God so without mincing words. If God and spiritual things bore you, admit it frankly. This advice will shock some squeamish saints, but it is altogether right nevertheless. God loves the guileless soul even when in his ignorance he is actually guilty of rashness in prayer. The Lord can soon cure his ignorance, but for insincerity no cure is known.

The basic artificiality of civilised human beings is hard to shake off. It gets into our very blood and conditions our thoughts, attitudes and relationships much more seriously than we imagine.

The desire to make a good impression has become one of the most powerful of all the factors determining human conduct. That gracious (and scriptural) social lubricant called courtesy has in our times degenerated into a completely false and phony etiquette that hides the true man under a shimmery surface as thin as the oil slick on a quiet pond. The only time some persons expose their real self is when they get mad.

With this perverted courtesy determining almost everything men say and do in human society, it is not surprising that it should be hard to be completely honest in our relations with God. It carries over as a kind of mental reflex and is present without our being aware of it. Nevertheless, it is extremely hateful to God. Christ detested it and condemned it without mercy when He found it among the Pharisees. The artless little child is still the divine model for all of us. Prayer will increase in power and reality as we repudiate all pretence and learn to be utterly honest before God as well as before men.

A great Christian of the past broke out all at once into a place of such radiance and victory as to excite wonder among his friends. Someone asked him what had happened to him. He replied simply that his new life of power began one day when he entered the presence of God and took a solemn vow never again to say anything to God in prayer that he did not mean. His transformation began with that vow and continued as he kept it.* **A. W. Tozer.**

I often say my prayers,
  But do I ever pray ?
Or do the wishes of my heart
  Suggest the words I say ?

'Tis useless to implore,
  Unless I feel my need;
Unless 'tis from a sense of want
  That all my prayers proceed.

I may as well kneel down
  And worship gods of stone,
As offer to the living God
  A prayer of words alone.

For words without the heart
  The Lord will never hear;
Nor will He ever those regard
  Whose prayers are insincere.

Lord ! teach me what I want,
  And teach me how to pray;
Nor let me e'er implore Thy grace,
  Not feeling what I say.

Selected

Prayer should be just what one feels, just what one thinks, just what one needs; and it should stop the moment it ceases to be the real expression of the need, the thought, and the feeling. **Beecher.**

*Excerpted from "Honesty in Prayer", in **God Tells The Man Who Cares**, by A. W. Tozer. Christian Publications, Inc., Harrisburg, Pa. 1970. Used by permission.

Answers
that cost

They said unto him, Grant unto us that we may sit, one on
thy right hand, and the other on thy left hand, in thy glory.
But Jesus said unto them, Ye know not what ye ask : can ye
drink of the cup that I drink of ? and be baptized with the
baptism that I am baptized with ? Mark 10 : 37, 38.

"Ye know not what ye ask !" How frequently we share these
uninformed petitions ! We, too, are asking for summits, and the
Lord answers our prayer, but it is so unlike the answer we
expected, for we find ourselves in heavy and burdensome
roads : but these are the first-fruits of grace, for they mark the
road that leads to the heights. I asked the gardener for a finer
hedge, closer in texture, a vesture without raggedness—no hole,
no rent or seam. And oh, what mutilations followed the
request, what clippings, what bleedings, what apparent waste !
A finer hedge had to be gained through the minister of
sacrifice.

You ask your Lord for sovereign joy. You know not what
you ask. Deeper joy is the issue of deeper refinement; and so,
instead of immediate joy, the Lord led you into the discipline
of severity, that the chords of your soul might be rendered
more sensitive, that so to their more delicate responsiveness
there might be given more exquisite delight. You asked for
sovereign beauty, spiritual beauty; you asked that "the beauty
of the Lord" might be upon you. You know not what you
asked; for between you and that sovereignty there lies
Gethsemane, with its exhausting but beautifying ministries of
intercessory prayer and sacrifice. You are asking for Heaven,
for a sovereign abode in the seats of the blest. You know not
what you ask !

> They climbed the steep ascent of heaven,
> Through peril, toil, and pain !

Heaven is the abode of the sacrificial, the gathering place of
crusaders; the secret of Heaven's glory is to be found in the

glorious characters we have fashioned on the way.

And so the gist of it all is this: thrones are for those who are fit to sit on them; we arrive at our throne when we are ready to rule. Sovereignties come to us in grace and sacrifice. It is well to lift our eyes to the hills, to the sublime human sovereignties which fill the vision in the sacred Word, and then in the strength of God's blessed grace and love set out for the difficult climb. For we have not to wait for our Lord's companionship until we reach a throne; He is with us while we are aspiring to it. He does not wait the warrior's arrival when the battle is over and won; He is with us on the field. Our companionship does not begin at the summit; it begins at the base. It is an interchange of cups from the start: "I will come in and sup with him, and he with me." **J. H. Jowett.**

There are not many things that have made me more vividly conscious of the antagonism of the old and the new nature, as the pouring out of such prayers as may involve suffering in their answers. There is a shrinking, and shuddering, and wincing. One trembles at the possible form the answer may take, and is almost ready to forego the desired spiritual blessing for very cowardice. Yet one prays on, and desire is stronger than fear, heaven is stronger than earth, and one pleads and wrestles to be "purified and made white", even if these are to be inseparable from the following words, "and tried": "that I may know Him, and the power of His resurrection", even if this be linked with "the fellowship of His sufferings". **F. R. Havergal.**

Neither will I offer burnt offerings unto the Lord my God of that which doth cost me nothing. **II Sam. 24:24.**

And he blessed him there . . . and he halted upon his thigh. **Gen. 32:29, 31.**

Ask out of
your poverty

Everyone that asketh receiveth. Matt. 7 : 8.

If thou knewest the gift of God . . . thou wouldest have asked of him, and he would have given thee. John 4 : 10.

Nothing is more difficult than to ask. We long, and desire, and crave, and suffer, but not until we are at the extreme limit will we ask. A sense of unreality makes us ask. We cannot bring ourselves up against spiritual reality when we like—all at once the staggering realisation dawns that we are destitute of the Holy Spirit, ignorant of all that the Lord Jesus stands for. The first result of being brought up against reality is this realisation of poverty, of the lack of wisdom, lack of the Holy Spirit, lack of power, lack of a grip on God. "If any of you lack wisdom, let him ask of God . . .", but be sure you do lack wisdom. Have you ever asked out of the depths of moral and spiritual poverty ?

If you realise you are lacking, it is because you have come in contact with spiritual reality. Don't put your reasonable 'blinkers' on again—'Preach us the simple gospel'; 'Don't tell me I have to be holy; that produces a sense of abject poverty, and it is not nice to feel abjectly poor.' Some people are poor enough to be interested in their poverty, and some of us are like that spiritually. 'Ask', means beg. A pauper does not ask from any desire save the abject, panging condition of his poverty.

Never deceive yourself by saying that if you do not ask you will not receive (cf. Matt. 5 : 45), although you will never receive from God until you have come to the stage of asking. Asking means that you have come into the relationship of a child of God, and you now realise with moral appreciation and spiritual understanding that "every good and perfect gift is from above, and cometh down from the Father of lights".

"Ye ask, and receive not," says the Apostle James, "because ye ask amiss." We ask amiss when we ask simply with the determination to outdo the patience of God until He gives us permission to do what we want to do. Such asking is mere sentimental unreality. And we ask amiss when we ask things from life and not from God, we are asking from the desire of self-realisation, which is the antipodes of Christian experience. The more we realise ourselves the less will we ask of God. Are we asking things of God or of life? We shall never receive if we ask with an end in view, we are asking not out of our poverty, but out of our lust. **Oswald Chambers.**

We are to show our appreciation of Christ by what we shall ask in His name. God gives us little to see if our Christ is little. Oh let us feel the necessity of showing the unsurpassable greatness of our Christ by the greatness of our supplications! Let us ask to be filled with the Spirit of God: filled with all the fullness of God; filled with the fruits of righteousness; filled with joy unspeakable.

What a world of wealth breaks upon the believer's perception when he supplicates the Father in the name of Christ! For, in order to show the significance of the name, he explores the treasuries of Christ's character and work. Every drop that fell from the brow of Christ, in Gethsemane, in the Pretorium and on Calvary, is found to be worth more at the mercy seat than all the mines of Golconda. The name of Christ is found to have an amplitude that stretches in every direction beyond the power of imagination to follow. But, sad to say, some Christians seem to have come to the end of their Christ. But what a foul reproach is this! What have you ever received from the throne of grace that you should think you had overdrawn your account and exhausted the virtue of Christ's name? **George Bowen.**

None of you asketh me. **John 16:5.**
They understood not . . . and were afraid to ask. **Mark 9:32.**
They feared to ask him of that saying. **Luke 9:45.**

Pray with size
ignoring faith

For there is no restraint to the Lord to save by many or by few. I Sam. 14 : 6.

God hath chosen the weak things of the world to confound the things which are mighty. I Cor. 1 : 27.

Faith is never mountain-moving because it moves mountains, but because it does not doubt God can move them, and will, at the need. Mountain-moving faith never tries, nor even thinks of trying to move mountains. It is fully convinced it could not if it tried, but it is also confident it need not try, for God will do it.

Mustard-seed faith is as undismayed at the opposition of a mountain as of a tree; because first, it does not reflect on its own size, is not abashed by self-consciousness, is unconcerned about its own insignificance; and secondly, because it does not make a business of measuring obstacles, has no eye for their relative size; for, as they are all finite, they are all of one size to faith—less than God, equally disproportioned to Him.

"Great" faith then, is neither self-absorbed, nor absorbed with circumstances, but is all absorbed with God. For it recognises that its only duty, yet its all-essential and bounden duty, in order to succeed, is simply to roll its little insignificant mustard-seed self up against the foot of the tree, or mountain, and lie there, looking up to God, watching and waiting in confident expectation till He removes it. **G. B. Peck.**

Childlikeness in prayer is essential. The adult rationalises, compares and then too often doubts. To a child, size means little. We knew a little girl who, while travelling through a game reserve in Africa with her parents, saw a lion too dangerously near. She begged her daddy to kill the king of beasts with a fly swatter. To her, daddy could deal with the lion as easily as with the insect. The same truth is portrayed by an extract from a speech given at the Edinburgh Missionary Conference, 1910: "We have lost the eternal youthfulness of Christianity, and have aged into calculating manhood. We seldom pray in earnest for the extraordinary, the limitless, the glorious. We seldom pray with real confidence for any good to the realisation of which we cannot imagine a way. And yet we suppose ourselves to believe in an infinite Father."

One of the special marks of the Holy Ghost in the Apostolic Church was the spirit of boldness. One of the most essential qualities of faith that is to attempt great things for God and expect great things from God, is holy audacity. Where we are dealing with a supernatural Being, and taking from Him things that are humanly impossible, it is easier to take much than little; it is easier to stand in a place of audacious trust than in a place of cautious, timid clinging to the shore. Likewise, seamen in the life of faith, let us launch out into the deep, and find that all things are possible with God, and all things are possible unto him that believeth. **A. B. Simpson.**

> Needed are men with a faith that's undauntable,
>   Faith like the prophets and martyrs of old,
> Reck'ning the dizziest heights all surmountable,
>   Digging thro' iron to get to the gold.
>
> Crossing the bridges they say are uncrossable,
>   Getting thro' jobs they say can't be got through;
> Men specialising in all that's impossible,
>   Doing the things people say they can't do.

Beware in your prayers, above everything else, of limiting God, not only by unbelief, but by fancying that you know what He can do. Expect unexpected things, "above all that we ask or think".

Each time, before you intercede, be quiet first, and worship God in His glory. Think of what He can do, and how He delights to hear the prayers of His redeemed people. Think of your place and privilege in Christ, and expect great things! **Andrew Murray.**

God's creative answers

If ye abide in me, and my words abide in you, ye shall ask what ye will, and it shall be done unto you. John 15 : 7.

All things were made by him. John 1 : 3.

Our belief in the possibility of prayer is based upon the declarations of Jesus, and behind His declarations there is Himself. If when I ask I never have; when I seek I cannot find; when I knock no door is opened to me, then either Christ was deceived or a deceiver. His teaching was most explicit. In this connection one quotation, perhaps the most remarkable of all, will suffice. "If ye abide in Me, and My words abide in you, ask whatsoever ye will, and it shall be done unto you." A careful examination of that passage makes it even more wonderful than appears at first sight. The word "ask" may with perfect accuracy be rendered "demand as your due". No violence will be done to the Lord's words if instead of "Whatsoever ye will" we read "whatsoever ye are inclined to". Yet again, the word translated "done", may be changed into "generated", and we have here, as it seems to me, the most stupendous statement regarding prayer ever uttered. It makes prayer limitless within limits. "If ye abide in Me, and My words abide in you" are the limits.

Let these be observed, then prayer becomes the method of co-operation with Deity. The life of true relation to Himself is one in which desire harmonises with the purposes of God, and which therefore demands an answer which is provided even though the creative force of Deity should be employed. If there is no answer to prayer, then these are the words of One Who was deceived, or was a deceiver—impossible alternatives despite a thousand newborn philosophies. Neither was He deceived, nor a deceiver. What He said is true though the heavens fall. Heaven and earth may pass away, but His word cannot. To deny the possibility of prayer is to deny the teaching of Jesus. To deny that teaching is to destroy Him.* **G. Campbell Morgan.**

Charles G. Trumbull has something most inspiring to say about this same verse: "When we pray according to God's will in faith in the name of Jesus, creative omnipotence springs forward to answer. When we remember that it was through Christ that every act of creation in the universe has always been wrought, it is not strange that nothing can prevent the answers to prayer when rightly offered in the name of that Creator. Thus it was that Jesus could say that the abiding Christian in whom His words abide, may ask whatsoever he will and it shall be **created** unto him. The word 'done' in that verse, 'and it shall be done unto you', is the Greek word **ginomai,** meaning to come into existence, receive being, be made. It is the same word as in John 1:3, 'All things were **made** through him'; the same word as in the passage, 'Command that these stones become bread'; and 'The water now become wine'.

"So as someone has truly said, Jesus urges us to ask for whatever we need, in His name, and He pledges us that He will answer even if, to do so, He needs to 'create into being' the thing that we need. It is worth while to pray; worth while to those for whom we pray; worth while to us; but best of all, worthwhile to God."

A born-again Christian prays God's promises into performances. **Sel.**

*From The Practice of Prayer by G. Campbell Morgan. (London: Hodder & Stoughton). Copyright 1907 by G. Campbell Morgan.

Faith stripped of human aids

He that had received the promises offered up his only begotten son, of whom it was said, That in Isaac shall thy seed be called. Heb. 11:17.

Abraham believed God. Rom. 4:3.

Abraham had "received" the promises of God, or, as J. N. Darby says, "adopted" them—made them his very own. Now, quite naturally, he looked upon Isaac as the means by which God would implement His promises.

Only He who sits as a refiner and purifier could know that to become the "father of the faithful", Abraham had still to learn the painful lesson that God needs nothing—needs no-one—to implement His own word. Anything or anyone Abraham imagined as being necessary beyond and outside of God Himself—any pledge or security other than God Himself—had to be done to death.

Out of this experience came Abraham's knowledge of God as Jehovah-jireh, the God who provides, out of Himself and from Himself alone.

Is not this what God is always teaching us? Having laid hold on some promise of God in real faith, do we not often begin to cast about for some way or thing, or person through which we may expect God to work? While all the time God wants us, as Matthew Henry says, to "depend upon the performance of the promise when all the ways leading up to it are shut up".

This was then, at least in part, what Abraham learned on the way up to Mount Moriah. **Elizabeth S. Bayles.**

> In vain our trembling conscience seeks
> Some solid ground to rest upon;
> With long despair our spirit breaks,
> 'Til we apply to Thee alone.
>
> **Isaac Watts**

"If any will dare to venture forth on the path of separation—cutting themselves aloof from all human aid and from all self-originated effort, content to walk alone with God with no help from any but Him—such will find that all the resources of the divine almightiness will be placed at their disposal . . . Why do we run to and fro for help of man when the power of God is within reach ?" **F. B. Meyer.**

At one stage of Christian experience we cannot believe unless we have some sign or some great manifestation or feeling. We feel our fleece, like Gideon, and if it is wet we are willing to trust God. This may be true faith but it is imperfect. It always looks for some feeling or some token beside the Word of God. It marks quite an advance when we trust God without feelings. It is blessed to believe without having any emotions.

There is a third stage of faith which even transcends that of Gideon and his fleece. The first phase believes when there are favourable emotions, the second believes when there is absence of feeling, but this third form of faith believes God and His Word when circumstances, emotions, appearances, people and human reason all urge to the contrary. May God give us faith to fully trust His Word though everything else witness the other way. **Anon.**

"As an eagle . . . fluttereth over her young, spreadeth abroad her wings, taketh them, beareth them on her wings, so the Lord alone did lead him."

"Fluttereth OVER"—the early stages of faith are a reaching upward, like the eaglets for their food when the mother bird is overhead. It is an older faith that learns to swing out into nothingness and drop down full weight on God —the broken-up nest of former "experiences" all left behind, nothing between us and the abyss but God Himself.

Trained faith is a triumphant gladness in having nothing but God—no nest, no foothold—nothing but Himself; a triumphant gladness in swinging out into the abyss, rejoicing in every emergency that is going to prove Him true. "The Lord alone"—that is trained faith. **Lilias Trotter.**

Faith,
the key to treasures

Who through faith . . . obtained promises. Heb. 11:33.
Let him ask in faith, nothing wavering. James 1:6.

"The promises are the veins in which the gold runs; it is a
work of faith to stamp this golden ore into ready money, for
the present necessity of the soul." **Hopkins.**

It is as important for us to know how to pray as it is to know
how to work. We are not told that Jesus ever taught His
disciples how to preach, but He taught them how to pray. He
wanted them to have power with God; then He knew they
would have power with man. In James we read, "If any of you
lack wisdom, let him ask of God . . . and it shall be given
him; but let him ask in faith, nothing wavering." So faith is
the golden key that unlocks the treasures of heaven. It was
the shield that David took when he met Goliath on the field;
he believed that God was going to deliver the Philistine into
his hands. Someone has said that faith could lead Christ about
anywhere; wherever He found it He honoured it. Unbelief sees
something in God's hand, and says, "I cannot get it". Faith
sees it, and says, "I will have it".

The new life begins with faith; then we have only to go on
building on that foundation. "I say unto you, what things soever
ye desire, when ye pray, believe that ye receive them, and ye
shall have them." But bear in mind, we must be in earnest
when we go to God.

Richard Sibbes puts it for us thus: "All is supernatural in
faith. The things we believe are above nature; the promises are
above nature; the worker of it, the Holy Ghost, is above nature;
and everything in faith is above nature. There must be a God
in Whom we believe, and a God through Whom we may know

that Christ is God—not only by that which Christ hath done, the miracles, which none could do but God, but also by what is done to Him. And two things are done to Him, which show that He is God—that is, faith and prayer. We must believe only in God, and pray only to God : but Christ is the object of both. Oh, what a strong foundation, what bottom and basis our faith hath ! There is God the Father, Son, and Holy Ghost, and Christ the Mediator. That our faith may be supported, we have Him to believe on Who supports Heaven and earth.

"There is nothing that can lie in the way of the accomplishment of any of God's promises, but it is conquerable by faith." **D. L. Moody.**

> Faith, mighty faith, the promise sees
>   And looks to that alone,
> Laughs at impossibilities
>   And cries **it shall be done !**

Charles Wesley

When we find anything promised in the Word of God, we are not to neglect to seek it because it is promised : but we are to pray for it on that very account. "Thus saith the Lord God; I will yet for this be inquired of by the house of Israel, to do it for them; I will increase them with men like a flock" (Ezek. 36 : 37). The promise is absolute; but the time of its fulfilment depends upon the prayers of His people. **B. T. Roberts.**

Mrs. Howard Taylor tells how Pastor Hsi, that courageous, godly Chinese pastor, learned to triumph by believing prayer : "He was so fearless. He did not hesitate to pray definitely about things, and then commit God, so to speak, to His own promises. 'Now that is settled', he would say : 'We have left it with the Heavenly Father. He will do it for us. Here is the promise'. Or if he believed he had been guided about a thing, he had no hesitation in saying just what the Lord had told him. People did not understand, and thought him boastful or irreverent. But it was rather David's spirit—'and now, Lord, do as Thou has said'; and a faith that was not afraid to let everybody know—'He will do it, for He has said so'. Sometimes he was wrong, but far more often it proved that he was right."

The boldness
of faith

Now, O Lord God . . . do as thou hast said. II Sam. 7:25.

Be of good cheer: for I believe God, that it shall be even as it was told me. Acts 27:25.

Prayer, when it prevails, has about it a boldness, a holy audacity, which reminds us of the prophet whose plea was, "Do not disgrace the throne of Thy glory!" (Jer. 14:21).

When a saint understands that prayer has three intercessors —the interceding Spirit within, the interceding suppliant, and the interceding Christ before the Throne—he feels himself but the channel through whom a current passes, whose source is the Holy Spirit in his heart, whose final outpour is through our great High Priest into the bosom of the Father. He loses sight of himself in the thought of the divine stream, and its spring and its ocean.

How can he but be bold? Prayer becomes no more mere lame and timid asking—it is claiming—and laying hold on blessing! Nay, it is waiting for and welcoming the blessing, as a returning stream from the heart of God, pouring back into and through the heart of the suppliant.

While he calls, God answers—there is a converse intercourse, intercommunication (Jer. 33:3). Prayer is not only speaking to God, but hearing Him speak in return. As a Japanese convert said, it is like the old-fashioned well, where one bucket comes down while another goes up—only, in this case, it is the full bucket that descends from Heaven. **A. T. Pierson.**

Faith is knowing that our Lord Jesus is Victor. That is to say it is not thinking about how much faith you have. It is thinking about Him! And it is not thinking so much about what He will do. It is thinking most about what He has done.

Jesus Christ is Victor. Faith is depending on that, or better yet, on Him! It is not working up your feelings, and saying, "I must believe"; not that. It is simply fixing my whole thought on Jesus, the Victor. There He is on the throne. That scarred, crowned, enthroned Lord Jesus—I have no doubt about Him! That is faith—looking to Him, resting on what He is, and what He has done, and what He says in His Word.

There's still another simple word to put in here that we may keep things in poise. A "taking" faith is a discerning faith. Those words "obey" and "abide" point to the close touch with the Master that lets us know what His plans are. The daily study of His Word reveals to us His will, and trains us to discern what His particular will is under the circumstance where you must act. Abiding makes us keen to know what we may take. The whole purpose underneath everything is to get His great loving will done. There must be a clear eye before there can be a taking hand.

As I step quietly on, under the gracious guidance of His Spirit, I am to "take" what I will, in His Name—life after life, man after man, gold after gold, strength renewed constantly for new work, anything and everything that is needed and that should be in His service. And because He is Victor, every hindrance must go, and will go, before the man who presses forward where He leads in His name.

Shall we go out and take, in Jesus' Name, what belongs to us by the right of His death and resurrection? **A. J. Gordon.**

Martin Luther had this boldness with God, and when Myconius, his helper in the Reformation, lay dying, this courageous man could not feel this was God's will. Luther replied as follows: "I command thee in the name of God to live because I still have need of thee in the work of reforming the church . . . The Lord will never let me hear that thou art dead, but will permit thee to survive me. For this I am praying . . . and may my will be done because I seek only to glorify the name of God!"

When Myconius received the letter he was unable to speak but he recovered and survived Luther by two months.

Bring out-sized buckets

And it came to pass, when the vessels were full, that she said unto her son, Bring me yet a vessel. And he said unto her, There is not a vessel more. And the oil stayed. II Kings 4 : 6.

Of his fullness have all we received. John 1 : 16.

Dan Crawford, a missionary to Africa, said, "My conception of prayer is that of buckets on an endless chain—they go up empty to express my need; they come down full, to express His bounty!"

We receive all spiritual gifts in proportion to our capacity, and the chief factor in settling the measure of our capacity is our faith.

Here on the one hand is the boundless ocean of the divine strength, unfathomable in its depth, full after all draughts, tideless and calm, in all its repose never stagnating; and on the other side is the empty aridity of our poor, weak natures.

Faith opens these to the influx of that great sea, and according to our faith, in the exact measure of our receptivity, does it enter into our hearts. In itself, the gift is boundless. It has absolutely no limit except the infinite fullness of the power which worketh in us.

But in reference to our possession it is bounded by our capacity. And though that capacity enlarges by the very fact of being filled and so every moment becomes greater through fruition, yet each moment it is the measure of our possession, and our faith is the measure of our capacity. Our power is God's power in us, and our faith is the power with which we grasp God's power and make it ours.

So then, in regard to God, our faith is the condition of our being strengthened with might by His Spirit. **Alexander McLaren.**

I once heard Dr. Berry give a charge to a young minister. In the course of that charge he said to the people, "You will get out of my young brother what you expect, and you will expect what you pray for". Then he used this homely but forceful illustration. Said he, "We were giving soup away lately to our poor people, and had issued general instructions that the lads who came to fetch the soup should bring with them a vessel that should hold about two quarts. I was at the soup kitchen one day, and saw a boy about ten years of age, ragged and dirty, but with eyes that flashed fire, going into the soup kitchen carrying a vessel that would hold at least three gallons. We could not for shame put two quarts into that." *G. Campbell Morgan.

Suppose that the man who was lame had come
To the Saviour by Galilee's shore,
And had asked for a cane to help him walk—
For a cane, and nothing more!

Suppose that the man who was blind from birth
Had asked for only a guide;
And had missed the wonder of Christ's dear face,
And the Heaven and earth beside!

Suppose that the woman who seemed rebuffed
Had turned away in despair;
Resigned to nurse her helpless child,
And the hurt of unanswered prayer!

Suppose they had been like you and me,
With their asking so fraught with doubt;
What sorrows and pains they would have retained—
What joys they'd have gone without!

Edith Bang

The reason why we obtain no more in prayer is because we expect no more. God usually answers us according to our own hearts. **Richard Alleine.**

*From The Practice of Prayer by G. Campbell Morgan. (London: Hodder & Stoughton).
Copyright 1907 by G. Campbell Morgan.

Battle tide's turning point

And he shewed me Joshua the high priest standing before the angel of the Lord, and Satan standing at his right hand to resist him. Zech. 3 : 1.

Resist the devil, and he will flee from you. James 4 : 7.

Your adversary the devil . . . walketh about, seeking whom he may devour : Whom resist. I Pet. 5 : 8, 9.

On maintaining the daily performance of closet duties the fate of the whole battle will turn. This your great adversary well knows. He knows that if he can beat you out of the closet, he will have you in his own power. You will be in the situation of an army cut off from supplies and reinforcements and will be obliged either to capitulate or to surrender at discretion.

He will, therefore, leave no means untried to drive or draw you from the closet. And it will be hard work to maintain that post against him and your own heart. On some occasions he will probably assail you with more violence when you attempt to read or pray than at any other time, and thus try to persuade you that prayer is rather injurious than beneficial. Again, he will withdraw and be quiet lest, if he should distress you with his temptations, you might be driven to the Throne of Grace for help.

If he can prevail upon us to be careless and stupid, he rarely will distress us. He will not disturb a false peace because it is a peace of which he is the author. But if he cannot succeed in lulling us to sleep, he will do all in his power to distress us. **E. Payson.**

> Stand your ground; your ghostly fears will fly.
> All hell trembles at a heaven-directed eye.

Men of prayer must be men of steel, for they will be assaulted by Satan even before they attempt to assault his kingdom.

Prayer which is merely putting in a request sheet to the Ruler of the Universe is but the smallest side of this many-faced truth. Like everything else in the Christian's life, prayer can become lopsided. Prayer is no substitute for work; equally true is it that work is no substitute for prayer. In his masterly but little-known work, The Weapon of Prayer, E. M. Bounds says, "It is better to let the work go by default than to let the praying go by neglect." Again he says, "The most efficient agents in disseminating the knowledge of God, in prosecuting His work upon the earth, and in standing as a breakwater against the billows of evil, have been praying church leaders. God depends upon them, employs them, and blesses them." **L. Ravenhill.**

Satan cannot deny but that great wonders have been wrought by prayer. As the spirit of prayer goes up, so his kingdom goes down. Satan's stratagems against prayer are three. First, if he can, he will keep thee from prayer. If that be not feasible, secondly, he will strive to interrupt thee in prayer. And, thirdly, if that plot takes not, he will labour to hinder the success of thy prayer. **Wm. Gurnall.**

From Andrew Bonar's diary we are enabled to enter into his conflict in prayer: "Satan has a special ill-will to praying people. Someone has said Satan's orders are, 'Fight not with small nor great, but only with the king of Israel' (Fight not with that saint nor that other, but only with the praying people).

"Tried yesterday and the night before to pray much. Often found Satan and the world striking in. Saw that, in Eph. 6:12, our position is said to be that of fighting our daily way through armies of devils who line the road."

The devil is aware that one hour of close fellowship, hearty converse with God in prayer, is able to pull down what he hath been contriving and building many a year. **Flavel.**

Binding
the Devil

Or else how can one enter into a strong man's house, and spoil his goods, except he first bind the strong man? and then he will spoil his house. Matt. 12 : 29.

Verily I say unto you, Whatsoever ye shall bind on earth shall be bound in heaven: and whatsoever ye shall loose on earth shall be loosed in heaven. Matt. 18 : 18.

The Church must learn this "binding" power of prayer, for it is written, "Whatsoever ye shall bind on earth shall be bound in heaven" (Matt. 18 : 18). And what can this "binding" mean except restraining the working of the enemy by appealing to the conquering power of Him who "was manifested to destroy the works of the devil". If you will only take the Word of God and search out this truth for yourself, you will understand that the victory of Calvary was not only a victory over sin, but victory over Satan, not only as a tempter, but as a hinderer, as a counterfeiter, as a deceiver, as a liar. And you will learn that you can have victory over the "strong man" in the victory of Calvary, and that too, not only for yourself, but for others you may stand with Jesus Christ in Victory for the mission fields of the world.

When men walk as "natural men" they are not much troubled about Satan, for he hides himself behind their natural condition. It is when man comes into a life of union with Christ and seeks to serve God that he knows the opposition of Satan. Directly the spirit is open to God, it is also open to the forces that are against God; when into the spirit of man the Holy Spirit comes and takes His place of indwelling, then immediately comes Satan as an angel of light, to try to counterfeit the Spirit of God. He is in a spiritual realm, and hence the forces that come against him are spiritual forces.

God means you to have victory. God intends your whole spirit and soul and body to be set free for His service. He means you to have your memory in full use, and entire control of your imagination, through the Name of Jesus. God means you to have your mind closed against the suggestions of the powers of darkness; to have your spirit so free that you can give the word of your testimony. The Holy Spirit of God enthroned in your spirit wants to use you, but cannot if you are oppressed, and heavy, and bound. Therefore ask God to give you the knowledge of liberty and victory in Christ, spirit, soul and body, so that you may walk in victory. God's children are yearning to be all that God wants them to be, and as far as their **wills** are concerned they do belong to God, and yet are in bondage. If they lived a life of steady victory, living in the spirit and praying in the spirit, the servants of God toiling in far-off lands would have a prayer force at the back of them that would tell with mighty power.

God has put into the hands of His children weapons for the warfare, weapons which are not of the flesh, but are "mighty through God to the pulling down of strongholds" (II Cor. 10 : 4). If people of God only knew, and laid hold of the weapons God has given them, they would arise with a shout of victory, instead of being depressed and talking about the blackness of the outlook on the world, the powers of darkness that have come down upon the whole Church of Christ could be shaken off. There are physical and nervous breakdowns, divisions injuring God's work, extraordinary tangles in Mission affairs, so great that some of God's saints do not know where to turn.

Here is the key : Take the victory of Calvary, and "bind the strong man" by prayer, so that he cannot hinder God's work. **Living Waters.**

A Christian warrior, Chas. E. Cowman, said : "The devil is not put to flight by a courteous request. He meets us at every turn, contends for every inch, and our progress has to be registered in heart's blood and tears."

> Blest, when assaulted by the tempter's power,
> The Cross my armour, and the Lamb my Tower,
> Kneeling I triumph—issuing from the fray
> A bleeding conqueror—my life a prey.

> **A. Monod**

God . . . giveth us the victory. **I Cor. 15 : 57.**

Marching on our knees

I prayed in my house, and, behold . . . Acts 10:30.
Yea, whiles I was speaking in prayer . . . Dan. 9:21.
When they had prayed, the place was shaken. Acts 4:31.

We engage the enemy—Satan and his forces—when we pray.
There it is the battle is fought, and the real victory won.
Christian work only succumbs to the enemy; it does not
engage him, or overcome his power unless we pray.

It is really only in the place of prayer that we wrestle against
principalities, against powers, the rulers of the darkness of this
world, and against spiritual wickedness in high places.

The entire armour is shaped for prayer. It is the real
battle-ground. Unless we learn to pray and wrestle there, we
shall get into the wrong battle and lose—the hot battle of
words and the clash of personalities.

The Lord had 120 "knockers", but He shut them all up to
prayer in the Upper Room. He taught them to do all their
knocking in prayer. Then He never had the problem of
"knocking" in His Church! There, in that Upper Room in
Jerusalem, He made them soldiers. There He mobilised them,
and there He also trained them for His warfare.

All through the Acts they march, after that, on their knees!
In almost every chapter they are praying. The new power they
have in the Spirit is like military power. For they witness and
win souls not only from sin, but from the bondage of the devil,
and that right in the very strongholds of heathenism. With
witnessing goes warfare. It is a constant battle for souls.
Armin R. Gesswein.

> The victories won by prayer,
>   By prayer must still be held;
> The foe retreats, but only when
>   By prayer he is compelled.

We will only advance in our evangelistic work as fast and as far as we advance on our knees. Prayer opens the channel between a soul and God; prayerlessness closes it. Prayer releases the grip of Satan's power; prayerlessness increases it. That is why prayer is so exhausting and so vital. If we believed it, the Prayer meeting would be as full as the Church. **Alan Redpath.**

And Andrew Bonar felt the fury of the devil: "Yesterday got a day to myself for prayer. With me every time of prayer, or almost every time, begins with a conflict, and often it is when I have been long done and am at my usual study that the tide seems to set in by way of answer, or earnest of an answer. For I scarcely ever have set apart special times for prayer and waiting upon the Lord without getting some such token of acceptance soon. O the folly of not praying more!"

Jean Corot, the French landscape painter, was small of build and gentle of nature. Occasion had never demanded this slightly-built artist to a show of strength until one day a bunch of ruffians decided he was an easy prey and so planned attack.

Corot threw himself into the attack and felled the largest ruffian. The others fled from the small man with the incredible punch. Jean Corot resuscitated the winded ruffian murmuring, "It's amazing. I never knew I was so strong."

Many Christians, gentle of manner and small of natural strength, never know the might they possess through the "greater One" who indwells them until they take the offensive against the enemy and attack. We are commanded in the Bible to resist the devil and promised "he will flee from you". We are encouraged to take the offensive because we are equipped for attack. The Christian was meant to take the enemy's hostages and gain territory for the Kingdom. As he does it, he realises the incredible strength of Him "Who is greater than he that is in the world".

If you hold daily communion with Him, and He touches you and you touch Him, you will go through the world like a man who is continually encompassed in impregnable armour. If God's hands are laid on your head, that head is helmeted; if God protects you, no arrow from the devil's bow can pierce your coat of mail. **Dr. A. T. Pierson.**

Fire upwards
on your knees

Lift up thy prayer . . . Lord bow down thine ear, and hear:
open, Lord, thine eyes, and see. II Kings 19 : 4, 16.

Unto thee, O Lord, do I lift up my soul. O my God, I trust in
thee : let me not be ashamed, let not mine enemies triumph
over me. Yea, let none that wait on thee be ashamed.
Psa. 25 : 1-3.

A story of the wars of the first Napoleon has often come back
to me. He was trying, in a winter campaign, to cut off the
march of the enemy across a frozen lake. The gunners were
told to fire on the ice and break it, but the cannon balls
glanced harmlessly along the surface. With one of the sudden
flashes of genius he gave the word. "Fire upwards!" and the
balls crashed down full weight shattering the whole sheet into
fragments, and the day was won. You can "fire upwards" in
this battle, even if you are shut out from fighting it face to
face. If God calls you there in bodily presence, you will never
be able to pray to any purpose, or work to any purpose either,
except there; but if He does not summon you, you can as truly,
as effectually, as prevailingly, do your share within the four
walls of your own room. "Said I not unto thee, that, if thou
wouldest believe, thou shouldest see the glory of God ?"
Lilias Trotter.

Some years ago in China, at a meeting of missionaries and
Chinese pastors, one of the Chinese pastors made a striking
address. He said that he and his brethren were more than
grateful to those who brought them the word of life and the
gospel of the Lord Jesus Christ, but yet, he said, there was
one thing more which missionaries should teach their
spiritual children.
   This new thing was to pray with authority, so that they might
know how to take their stand in faith before the throne of God,
and rebuke the forces of evil, hold steady and firm, and gain
the victory over them.

That same need is tremendously evident today in the experiences of all who are seeking to walk closely with the Lord, and to stand for Him in the face of increasing opposition.

Some have spoken of this as "throne prayer"—praying with one's hand touching the throne of God. **T. Stanley Soltau.**

It must be remembered that there are "spiritual wickednesses" at the back of all confusion and discord in the work of God. The servant of Christ must, therefore, practically recognise that his warfare is with these satanic beings and must be waged on his knees. How blessed that this . . . lays it open to the weakest of us to prevail in matters which would otherwise be entirely beyond our strength and wisdom. **D. E. Hoste.**

From the South African Pioneer comes this illuminating account of the power of prayer to bind "the strong man" and render ineffectual his emissaries :

Our South Africa General Mission office in Glasgow is in a building owned by the C.S.S.M. and shared by a number of missionary societies. Across the road is a Spiritualist church. On our side of the road a series of special prayer meetings was being held. A note was sent from the Spiritualist church requesting that the prayer meetings be stopped because their medium could not get through. How many demons may be prevented from getting through to stir up trouble if only we learn to continue steadfastly in prayer.

The man who is mighty in prayer may be a wall of fire around his country, her guardian angel and her shield . . . If any man here should venture to say that he prays as much as he ought, as a student, I should gravely question his statement; and if there be a minister, deacon, or elder present who can say that he believes he is occupied with God in prayer to the full extent to which he might be, I should be pleased to know him. I can only say, that if he can claim this excellence, he leaves me far behind, for I can make no such claim; I wish I could . . . If we are not more negligent than others, this is no consolation to us; the shortcomings of others are no excuses for us. **Spurgeon.**

An authoritative notice to quit

Begin to possess, that thou mayest inherit his land. Deut. 2 : 31.
They could not enter in because of unbelief. Heb. 3 : 19.

Faith and works must never be divorced, for indolence will reap no harvest in the spiritual world. I think the principle will be found to hold in any case where the prayer of faith is offered, but there is no doubt that it always holds good in cases where the strongholds of Satan are attacked, where the prey is to be wrested from the strong.

Think of the children of Israel under Joshua. God had given them the land of Canaan—**given** it to them, notice, by free grace—but see how they had to fight when once they commenced actually to take possession !

Satan's tactics seem to be as follows. He will first of all oppose our breaking through to the place of a real, living faith, by all means in his power. He detests the prayer of faith, for it is an authoritative "notice to quit". He does not so much mind rambling, carnal prayers, for they do not hurt him much. This is why it is so difficult to attain to a definite faith in God for a definite object.

We often have to strive and wrestle in prayer (Eph. 6 : 10-12) before we attain this quiet, restful faith. And until we break right through and **join hands with God** we have not attained to real faith at all. Faith is a gift of God—if we stop short of it we are using mere fleshly energy or will-power, weapons of no value in this warfare. Once we attain to a real faith, however, all the forces of hell are impotent to annul it. What then ? They retire and muster their forces on this plot of ground which God has pledged Himself to give us, and contest every inch of it. The real battle begins when the prayer of faith has been offered. But, praise the Lord ! we are on the winning side.

Let us read and re-read the tenth chapter of Joshua, and never talk about defeat again. Defeat, indeed! No, Victory! Victory! Victory! **J. O. Fraser.**

Speaking of the bold adventuring of the early church, C. T. Studd says: "Ten days they waited for their armament and orders. Both came together, the same day, early, suddenly. So well prepared were they and so eager for the fray, that by 9 o'clock of the same morning war had been declared and the first battle begun. Ere night fell, 3,000 of the enemy had surrendered, bowed the knee to the Christian Commander, and enlisted to fight under His Banner.

"Such was the result of Faith. The sights those days in Jerusalem were some of the strangest ever seen. The few were fighting the many! The fools were teaching the wise! The weak were tackling the strong! The Ecclesiastical pillars were being defied by an insignificant group of laymen, unlearned, unschooled and unordained! But the most delicious thing of all was that the poor, weak lay fools were ever the victors and their army always increasing.

"Being the age of Faith it was also that of Miracles and among the many marvels seen there were none greater than these:—The man who had been scared out of his wits by a housemaid and had lied to save his life, was now to be seen courting death by boldly confessing Christ and telling the truth. He who had sat and warmed himself was now seen warming others and especially the priests with good, hot spicy food.

"They who had, but a few weeks before, in fear of their lives, denied and forsaken the Christ and fled, after being scourged and threatened with death, were joyfully congratulating themselves that they had been counted worthy to suffer for HIS Name's sake. The Priests were arresting, imprisoning and scourging the disciples of Christ for preaching His Name without their ordination or licence, while God was busy liberating, encouraging and working with them. No wonder the Gospel spread like wildfire!"

Time to consult

David inquired of the Lord, saying, Shall I go up to the Philistines? wilt thou deliver them up into mine hand? And the Lord said unto David, Go up: for I will doubtless deliver the Philistines into thine hand. II Sam. 5 : 19.

And she went to enquire of the Lord. Gen. 25 : 22.

Prophets have enquired and searched diligently. I Pet. 1 : 10.

There are two principal elements in the strategy of prayer. The first is unhurried communion. To take time to examine a spiritual situation in the presence of God is the initial condition for making prayer effective.

In the great warfare of Christian witness, quietness of spirit is demanded to develop a true, vigorous, healthy prayer force, and prevent the nervous strain which so frequently brings to an end the service of a believer.

In Christian life the peril is to be always "on the move", especially in relation to prayer. To be hurried, either in word or act, is never a sign of the leading of the Spirit of God, but it is not the least effective of satanic strategies in the spiritual conflict. To push the believer to speech or effort, without giving time for prayer to see the way of God, is one of his favourite strategems. And many tragedies, great and small, in Christian experience are caused by the driving force of the devil.

It will never be unwise to suspect every impulse to act on the spur of the moment, and to take time to catch the right vision of the matter which concerns us. "God works slowly", as Bishop Westcott wrote. Never in a hurry, the unresting, and yet unwearied God waits long to complete His preparation. Then, in due season, He finishes the work of ages in a moment. In a material struggle it is imperative to have a council of war, when plans for offence or defence are prepared. In every Church and association of workers, God needs to find His staff, who can enter into consultation with Him, and in His light see light.

The other element in the strategy of prayer is to discover what Dr. Andrew Murray has called "the storm centre on the battlefield". To find that out, in a life or a work, is the condition of victory. What it may be will be revealed by the Holy Spirit in the spiritual Council Chamber. When light breaks on it, prayer must be focused upon it, and definite steps taken to stop the power of the devil, and bring the whole situation within the sphere of the Cross, through the might of the Holy Spirit. **Gordon B. Watt.**

I owe much to the practice which I am here emphasising, namely, that of breaking away entirely from the presence of men and shutting oneself in alone with God and His truth for the purpose of self-examination, prolonged reflection, communion, and resolution. In reading Hanna's "Memoirs of Dr. Chalmers", that great preacher of Scotland, I discovered that for years he had the practice of spending a day each month in this vital manner. That explains the secret of his shaking the great city of Glasgow and exerting an influence felt there to this day.***J. R. Mott.**

"A restful realisation of the Lord's companionship," wrote Dr. Jowett, "has been the characteristic of men whose religious activity has been forceful, influential, and fertile in the purpose of the Kingdom. At the very heart of all their labours, in the very centre of their stormiest days, there is a sphere of sure and restful intimacy with the Lord . . . Get a man who is restfully intimate with his Lord, and you have a man whose force is tremendous ! Such men move in apparent ease, but it is the ease that is linked with the infinite; it is the very rest of God. They may be engaged in apparent trifles, but even in the doing of trifles there emerge the health-giving currents of the Kingdom of God."

*From Confronting Young Men with the Living Christ by J. R. Mott.
(London: Hodder & Stoughton).

Prayer's wider horizons

For since the beginning of the world men have not heard, nor perceived by the ear, neither hath the eye seen, O God, beside thee, what he hath prepared for him that waiteth for him.
Isa. 64 : 4.

While we look not at the things which are seen, but at the things which are not seen : for the things which are seen are temporal; but the things which are not seen are eternal.
II Cor. 4 : 18.

By prayer, God ordained that man should break out of his material imprisonment of the seen in order to view the immensity of God and the vastness of His resources. Our viewpoint becomes restricted by our very soulishness, but in prayer the spirit is given opportunity to explore wider horizons.

Many a one of God's children has become so shut in that he can see only his family, his work, his church or his organisation. To such a one often what appears an imprisoning circumstance comes. Perhaps it is an illness that gives the pause needed for viewing the infiniteness of God. Sometimes a servant of God has been imprisoned within a narrow cell, and for the first time has been enabled to really meditate.

Geoffrey Bull, missionary to Tibet, learned in a Communist prison cell what he had not had time to learn in his arduous missionary efforts. The deeper meaning of God's Word and His purposes opened up to his view during those long, torturous hours of solitary confinement. Reading his books one is enriched by his spiritual grasp of what otherwise would seem very ordinary truth.

"Abraham's tent was changed for the sky," said J. H. Jowett. "Abraham sat moodily in his tent; God brought him forth beneath the stars. And that is always the line of divine leading. He brings us forth out of our small imprisonments and He sets our feet in a large place. He desires for us height and breadth of view. He wishes us, I say, to exchange the tent of the material for the sky of the spirit, and to live and move in great spacious thought of His purpose and will."

There is a fable told by Mrs. W. Bitzer of two tortoises—one blind who had lived all his life in a well; the other had been a native of the ocean. In the course of his travels, the ocean-going tortoise tumbled into the well. The inhabitant of the well asked the newcomer from whence he had come.

"From the sea," answered the tortoise.

The tortoise of the well swam round two-thirds of his domain and queried if the sea was as big as that.

"Much larger than that," replied the newcomer.

"Well, then, is the sea as large as the whole well?"

"Larger."

"If that is so," exclaimed the tortoise of the well in astonishment, "then how big is the sea?"

"Since you never have known any other water than that of your well," answered the tortoise of the sea, "your capability of understanding the subject is proportionately small. As to the ocean, though you were to spend many years in its water, you never would be able to explore the half of it. Nor could you ever hope to reach its limit. The ocean positively cannot be compared with this well of yours."

"It is impossible that there could be a larger body of water than this well," remarked the blind tortoise stubbornly. "You are simply praising your native place in vain words."

He who has no vision of Eternity will never get a true hold of Time. **T. Carlyle.**

Live near to God, and so all things will appear to you little in comparison with eternal realities. **Robert Murray McCheyne.**

Prayer—the time exposure of the soul

But we all, with open face beholding as in a glass the glory of the Lord, are changed into the same image from glory to glory, even as by the Spirit of the Lord. II. Cor. 3 : 18.

Let the beauty of the Lord our God be upon us. Psa. 90 : 17.

Prayer is the time-exposure of the soul to God, in which the image of God is formed on the soul.

We try in our piety to practise instantaneous photography. One minute for prayer will give us a vision of the image of God, and we think that enough. Our pictures are poor because our negative is weak. We do not give God a long enough sitting to get a good likeness. We do not acquaint ourselves with Him. We do not fill ourselves with His life.

The incarnation is not merely the indwelling of the Spirit of God once for three short years in a human life—it is the indwelling of God in all His children. It is only as we reflect, as from a mirror, the image of God that we are transformed into the same image from glory to glory. **Great Thoughts.**

It is wonderful how soon we become like what we love and pursue . . . Hearts and lives take on the complexion of the people and things which predominate in daily experience.

So let it be in your relation to the Lord Jesus, Who indeed is the true Light of souls. Think of Him. Imitate Him. Ask continually what He would wish. Saturate your mind with His words and teaching. Live up to His will so far as you know it. Obey Him to the uttermost. And there will come a growing resemblance between you and Him. You will be transformed, as you behold, into His likeness. Men, as they come into contact with you, will be constrained to acknowledge you as a child of the Light.

Oh to descend into the world each morning as sunbeams

from the fount of day !—bearing with us something of the beauty of the world from which we come; living lives as transparent, as beautiful, as unobtrusive, and as helpful in our measure as His was, from Whom we have received all we have and are. **F. B. Meyer.**

"Looking unto Jesus,"—that conveys the idea of rigidly shutting out other things in order that one supreme light may fill the eye and gladden the soul. If you do not carefully drop the black curtains round the little chamber, and exclude all the side lights, as well as the other objects from the field of vision, there will be no clear impression of the beloved face upon the sensitive plate. "It must be in the darkness that the image is transferred to the heart." **Alexander Maclaren.**

To receive the law, Moses was in the Mount for 40 days and 40 nights (Ex. 24 : 18, Deut. 9 : 9-11). Dr. Joseph Parker's apt comment on Moses' somewhat long absence from the earth is worth reciting : "The few commandments which we once called the Law could be written in less than a minute each; it was not the handwriting but the heart-writing that required the time."

Time spent in quiet prostration of soul before the Lord is most invigorating. David "sat before the Lord"; it is a great thing to hold these sacred sittings; the mind being receptive, like an open flower, drinking in the sunbeams, or the sensitive photographic plate accepting the image before it. Quietude, which some men cannot abide, because it reveals their inward poverty, is a palace of cedar to the wise, for along its hallowed courts the King in His beauty deigns to walk. Priceless as the gift of utterance may be, the practice of silence in some aspects far excels it. I am persuaded that we most of us think too much of speech, which after all is but the shell of thought. Quiet contemplation, still worship, unuttered rapture, these are mine when my best jewels are before me. Brethren, rob not your heart of the deep sea joys; miss not the far-down life, by for ever babbling among the broken shells and foaming surges of the shore. **Spurgeon.**

The encroaching wilderness

I beheld, and, lo, the fruitful place was a wilderness. Jer. 4 : 26.

He will make her wilderness like Eden, and her desert like the garden of the Lord. Isa. 51 : 3.

"Man was made to dwell in a garden," says Dr. Harold C. Mason, "but through sin he has been forced to dwell in a field, a field which he has wrested from his enemies by sweat and tears, and which he preserves only at the price of constant watchfulness and endless toil. Let him but relax his efforts for a few years and the wilderness will claim his field again. The jungle and the forest will swallow his labours and all his loving care will have been in vain."

Every farmer knows the hunger of the wilderness, that hunger which no modern farm machinery, no improved agricultural methods, can ever quite destroy. No matter how well prepared the soil, how well kept the fences, how carefully painted the buildings, let the owner neglect for a while his prized and valued acres and they will revert again to the wild and be swallowed up by the jungle or the wasteland. The bias of nature is toward the wilderness, never toward the fruitful field.

To the alert Christian this fact will be more than an observation of interest to farmers; it will be a parable, an object lesson setting forth a law that runs through all the regions of our fallen world, affecting things spiritual as well as things material. We cannot escape the law that would persuade all things to remain wild or to return to a wild state after a period of cultivation. What is true of the field is true also of the soul, if we are but wise enough to see it.

The moral bent of the fallen world is not toward godliness but definitely away from it. "Is this vile world a friend to grace," asks the poet rhetorically, "to help me on to God?" The sad answer is no, and it would be well for us to see that each new Christian learns this lesson as soon as possible after his conversion. We sometimes leave the impression that it is possible to find at an altar of prayer, once and for all, purity of heart and power to assure victorious living for the rest of our days. How wrong this notion is has been proved by countless numbers of Christians through the centuries.

The truth is that no spiritual experience, however revolutionary, can exempt us from temptation; and what is temptation but the effort of the wilderness to encroach upon our new-cleared field? The purified heart is obnoxious to the devil and to all the forces of the lost world. They will not rest until they have won back what they have lost. The jungle will creep in and seek to swallow up the tiny areas that have been made free by the power of the Holy Ghost. Only watchfulness and constant prayer can preserve those moral gains won for us through the operations of God's grace.

The neglected heart will soon be a heart overrun with worldly thoughts; the neglected life will soon become a moral chaos; the church that is not jealously protected by mighty intercession and sacrificial labours will before long become the abode of every evil bird and the hiding place for unsuspected corruption. The creeping wilderness will soon take over that church that trusts in its own strength and forgets to watch and pray.* **A. W. Tozer.**

To the man who never prays . . . there is little hope that a convincing religious experience will ever come. But to the man who prays habitually (not only when he feels like it—that is one of the snares of religion—but also when he does not feel like it) Christ is sure to make Himself real. **James Stewart.**

* Excerpted from "The Hunger of the Wilderness", in **The Root of the Righteous**, by A. W. Tozer. Christian Publications, Inc., Harrisburg, Pa. 1955. Used by permission.

To the fountain

They have forsaken me the fountain of living waters, and hewed them out cisterns, broken cisterns, that can hold no water. Jer. 2 : 13.

I will give unto him that Is athirst of the fountain of the water of life freely. Rev. 21 : 6.

We have held more communion with man than with God! We have given a greater prominence to man's writings, man's opinions, man's systems in our studies—than to the Word of God (Isa. 8 : 20; I Thess. 2 : 13). We have drunk more out of human cisterns than divine.

Hence the mould and fashion of our spirits, our lives, our words, have been derived more from man than from God. We must study the Bible more. We must steep our souls in it. We must not only lay it up within us, but transfuse it through the whole texture of the soul.

We have not been men of prayer. The spirit of prayer has slumbered among us. The closet has been too little frequented and delighted in. We have allowed business, study or active labour to interfere with our closet-hours. And the feverish atmosphere in which both the church and the nation are enveloped has found its way into our prayer closets, disturbing the sweet calm of its blessed solitude.

Sleep, company, idle visiting, foolish talking and jesting, idle reading, unprofitable occupations (radio, television, etc.) engross time that should be redeemed for prayer and soul winning.

Prayerlessness is a sin that can be repented of and blood-cleansed—like other sins. Why is there so little anxiety to get time to pray? Why is there so little forethought in the laying out of time and employment so as to secure a large portion of each day for prayer? Why is there so much speaking, yet so little prayer?

Why is there so much running to and fro to meetings,

conventions, fellowship gatherings and yet so little time for prayer ? Brethren, why so many meetings with our fellow men and so few meetings with God ? **A. Bonar.**

Sister Eva, Mother of the Friedenshort Sisterhood, who gave so freely of her life's strength to the strengthless, poor and weak said : "The lack of quiet time of meditation and inward communion with God, drawing the Water of Life from the Fountainhead, is the chief cause of so much spiritual weakness and stunted growth . . . What would our life be if we only understood how to use aright this privilege of Grace !"*

And D. L. Moody, known to us all for his indefatigable efforts at soul-saving said : "Next to the wonder of seeing my Saviour will be, I think, the wonder that I made so little use of the power of prayer."

Vital and uninterrupted contact with our Heavenly Father is the most wonderful thing in the world.
Lieut.-General Sir William Dobbie.

> O Mighty God, Thy matchless power
>   Is ever new and ever young,
> And firm endures, while endless years,
>   Their everlasting circles run.
>
> From Thee, the ever-flowing spring,
>   Our souls shall drink a fresh supply;
> While such as trust their native strength
>   Shall melt away, and droop, and die.
>
> **Isaac Watts**

Blessed are they . . . that seek him with the whole heart.
Psa. 119 : 2.
For the pastors . . . have not sought the Lord : therefore they shall not prosper, and all their flocks shall be scattered.
Jer. 10 : 21.

*From "The True Meaning of Life" by Sister Eva of Friedenshirt. (London: Hodder and Stoughton) Copyright 1937 by China Inland Mission.

Immersing ourselves in prayer

Thus saith the Lord . . . Seek ye me, and ye shall live. Amos. 5 : 4.

Seek the Lord, and ye shall live. Amos 5 : 6.

I am as certain as I am standing here, that the secret of much mischief to our own souls, and to the souls of others, lies in the way that we stint, and starve, and scamp our prayers by hurrying over them. Prayer worth calling prayer: prayer that God will call true prayer and will treat as true prayer, takes far more time, by the clock, than one man in a thousand thinks.

Take good care lest you take your salvation far too softly and far too cheaply. If you find your life of prayer to be always so short, and so easy, and so spiritual, as to be without cost and strain and sweat to you, you may depend upon it, you are not yet begun to pray. As sure as you sit there, and I stand here, it is just in this matter of time in prayer that so many of us are making shipwreck of our own souls, and the souls of others.

Were some of us shut up in prison like Paul, I believe we have grace enough to become in that sequestered life men of great and prevailing prayer. And, perhaps, when we are sufficiently old and set free from business, and are sick tired of spending our late nights eating and drinking and talking: when both the church and the world are sick tired of us and leave us alone and forget us, we may find time for prayer and may get back the years of prayer those canker-worms have eaten. **Alexander Whyte.**

"To pray as God would have us pray," wrote Samuel Chadwick, "is the greatest achievement on earth. Such a life of prayer costs. It takes time. Hurried prayers and muttered Litanies can never produce souls mighty in prayer. Learners give hours regularly each day that they may become proficient in art and mechanism. All praying saints have spent hours every day in prayer . . . In these days there is no time to pray; but without time, and a lot of it, we shall never learn to pray. It ought to be possible to give God one hour out of twenty-four all to Himself." *

It was not easy for this busy man, Samuel Chadwick, to make time for prayer. A glimpse into his personal prayer life is given in the following: "I went apart three times a day and prayed in spirit all the time between. The habit of three times a day was not easy. The dinner hour was short, the family was large, and the house small, but I managed."

Charles Kingsley tells of Turner, the greatest Nature-painter of any age. He spent hours upon hours in mere contemplation of Nature without using his pencil at all. "It is said of him that he was known to spend a whole day sitting upon a rock, and throwing pebbles into a lake; and, when at evening his fellow-painters showed him their day's sketches, and rallied him upon having done nothing, he answered them, 'I have done this at least—I have learned how a lake looks when pebbles are thrown into it.' "

Henry Martyn, a brilliant scholar, linguist and missionary to India sensed a real danger in giving too little time to prayer: "May the Lord, in mercy, save me from setting up an idol of any sort in His room, as I do by preferring a work professedly for Him to communion with Him. How obstinate the reluctance of the natural heart to God. But, O my soul, be not deceived, the chief work on earth is to obtain sanctification and to walk with God."

*From "The Path of Prayer" by Samual Chadwick. (London: Hodder & Stoughton). Copyright 1951 by Samual Chadwick. Copyright 1956 by Hodder & Stoughton Limited.

Waiting,
a proof of our faith

Let not them that wait on thee, O Lord God of hosts, be ashamed for my sake: let not those that seek thee be confounded. Psa. 69 : 6.

The Lord is good unto them that wait for him, to the soul that seeketh him. Lam. 3 : 25.

Wait! It is but a monosyllable; yet it is fuller of meaning than any other word in the language, and it is applicable to all ages and to all circumstances. At the first slight view, merely to "wait", seems so simple a thing, that it is scarcely entitled to be called a grace; and yet larger promises are made to it than to any other grace, except faith; and hardly, indeed, with that exception, for the grace of "waiting" is part of the grace of faith—is a form of faith—is, as some would describe it, an effect of faith, or, more strictly, one of its most fruitful manifestations.

Great and singular is the honour which God has set upon patient waiting for Him. Man, seeing not as God sees, sets higher value upon his fellows' active works—the bright deeds of days or hours. God values these also; but He does not assign them the same pre-eminence which man assigns them; He does not allow them a pre-eminence over that constant and long enduring struggle with the risings of the natural mind, which is evinced in long and steady waiting under all discouragements for Him, in the assured conviction that He will come at last for deliverance and protection, although his chariot wheels are so long in coming.

Active virtue brings present reward with it. Apart from the encouraging applause it obtains from some, it is attended with a pleasurable excitation of spirits, in the mere sense of action, as well as in the hopes and aspirations connected with it. There is nothing of this in mere patient waiting, day after day, through long years perhaps—and it may be in dust and ashes —until the Lord shall manifest towards us His love, His sympathy, His care. But to rest thus in the assured conviction that He will do so is a tribute rendered by faith to His honour, a tribute which He holds in most high esteem, and which He does most abundantly recompense. This recompense such faith needs; for it is a quality of the Christian character which, as God only can truly understand it, finds little encouragement but from Him. It receives, less than any other, the outer sustainment of man's approval and admiration. **John Kitto.**

"He that believeth shall not make haste." That is no easy lesson for you or me to learn; but I honestly think ten years would be well spent, and we should have our full value for them, if we thoroughly learned it in them . . . Moses seems to have been taken aside for forty years to learn it . . . Meanwhile let us beware alike of the haste of the impatient, impetuous flesh, and of its disappointment and weariness. **Hudson Taylor.**

Seems we're always in a hurry,
  In our age of speed today.
Everything must be kept moving,
  Till there's little time to pray.
Not much time to worship Jesus,
  Not much time our hearts to search—
Not much time to read the Bible—
  Little time for God and church.

We must learn the art of waiting,
  Slow our pace, take time for prayer—
Ask the Lord to give us patience
  In our home and everywhere.
There are peace and quiet living
  Which only come through grace divine.
Please don't forget, God never hurries,
  And He's always there on time.

F. W. Davis

Though it (the vision) tarry, wait for it; because it will surely come. **Hab. 2 : 3.**

Consulation
with highest wisdom

And Abraham answered and said, Behold now, I have taken upon me to speak unto the Lord, which am but dust and ashes. Gen. 18 : 27.

At the door of the tabernacle . . . where I will meet you, to speak there unto thee. Exodus 29 : 42.

Prayer keeps the communication open between the Head and the members; it is the messenger that goes from earth to Heaven, and returns with all necessary blessings from thence. Beware, then, of neglecting this necessary duty. Pray in faith, pray in the name of Christ, pray without ceasing; and beg of Christ to teach you to pray aright, that you may ask and receive, and then your joy shall be full. **Selected.**

Dr. Austin Phelps says : "I come to my devotions this morning on an errand of real life. This is no romance, and no farce. I do not come here to go through a form of words; I have no hopeless desires to express. I have an object to gain; I have an end to accomplish. This is a business in which I am about to engage. An astronomer does not turn his telescope to the skies with a more reasonable hope of penetrating those distant heavens, than I have of reaching the mind of God, by lifting up my heart at the Throne of Grace. This is the privilege of my calling of God in Christ Jesus. Even my faltering voice is now to be heard in Heaven; and it is to put forth a new power there, the results of which only God can know and only eternity can develop."

Prayer is not a consultation with the highest wisdom which this world can supply. It is not intercourse with an angel or a spirit made perfect. But it is an approach to the living God. It is access to the high and holy One who inhabiteth eternity. It is detailing in the ear of Divine sympathy every sorrow. It is consulting with Divine Wisdom on every difficulty. It is asking from Divine resources the supply of every want. And this not once in a lifetime, or for a few moments on a stated day of each year, but at any moment, at every time of need. **James Hamilton, D.D.**

"Prayer," says William Law, "is the nearest approach to God, and the highest enjoyment of Him of which we are capable in this life."

Phillips Brooks was once crossing the Atlantic, and a young friend of his wanted to see him. He searched for him on deck and in the state rooms, and could not find him. Then he went to his cabin and knocked, but got no answer. Gently opening the door, he saw the bishop inside, prostrate on the floor, and heard him say, "Lord Jesus, Thou hast filled my life with peace and gladness. To look into Thy face is earth's most exquisite joy." **W. Y. Fullerton.**

The word "prayer", both in Scriptural and in popular usage, denotes a somewhat comprehensive exercise throughout which there is a personal approach of the soul to God. Prayer may be engaged in with others, in public or family worship, or it may be an individual and private act. In either case, and whether the words be audibly repeated or silently thought, the man speaks with God, mind with mind, heart with heart.

It is not mere meditation upon God but a direct address to Him. Man talks with God. **Wm. Patton.**

The Old Testament is a book of recorded conversations—of God with man, and man with God. The expressions, "The Lord saith", "Thus saith the Lord", and "God spake", occur no less than 1904 times in the thirty-nine books.

When I called, none did answer; when I spake, they did not hear. **Isa. 66 : 4.**

> Far from my thoughts, vain world begone;
>   Let my religious hours alone;
> Fain would mine eyes my Saviour see;
>   I wait a visit, Lord, from Thee.

The perils
of the busy man

And the men took of their victuals, and asked not counsel at the mouth of the Lord. Josh. 9 : 14.

They waited not for his counsel. Psa. 106 : 13.

I will look unto the Lord; I will wait for the God of my salvation : my God will hear me. Micah 7 : 7.

The whole habit of life of the modern world has been changed, and for the worst spiritually, by two inventions, rapid locomotion and brilliant artificial lights. By the latter night can be turned into day; the world sits up late and cannot rise early; the evident rule of the Creator for His creatures is disregarded by man, and one inevitable result is that, while birds and beasts go on without nervous disorders, the human race gets more and more neurotic and independable.

The Christian who willingly or thoughtlessly conforms to the world in this one particular of late retiring and rising late, will scarcely be heavenly minded like Jesus was on earth : for disregard of the will of God in one matter will induce general disregard, and general walking by the will of man, and thus the spirit and tone of the believer will be that of earth and not Heaven. In his deeply instructive biography, "George Muller of Bristol", A. T. Pierson wrote :

On April 29th, Mr. Muller left for Bristol. On the journey he was dumb, having no liberty in speaking for Christ or even in giving away tracts and this led him to reflect. He saw that the so-called "work of the Lord" had tempted him to substitute action for meditation and communion. He had neglected that "still hour" with God which supplies to spiritual life its breath and its bread. No lesson is more important for us to learn, yet how slow are we to learn it; that for the lack of habitual seasons set apart for devout meditation upon the Word of God and for prayer, nothing else will compensate.

We are prone to think, for example, that converse with Christian brethren and the general round of Christian activity, especially when we are much busied with preaching the Word and visits to inquiring or needy souls, make up for the loss of aloneness with God in the secret place. We hurry to a public service with but a few minutes of private prayer, allowing precious time to be absorbed in social pleasures, restrained from withdrawing from others by a false delicacy, when to excuse ourselves for needful communion with God would have been perhaps the best witness possible to those whose company was holding us unduly! How often we rush from one public engagement to another without any proper interval for renewing our strength in waiting on the Lord, as though God cared more for the quantity than the quality of our service!

Here Mr. Muller had the grace to detect one of the foremost perils of a busy man in this day of insane hurry. He saw that if we are to feed others we must be fed; and that even public and united exercises of praise and prayer can never supply that food which is dealt out to the believer only in the closet— the shut-in place with its closed door and open window, where he meets God alone. * **G. H. Lang.**

Each man must fight for his prayer life. The more sacred and potential a spiritual practice or observation is, the more do our spiritual enemies seek to rob it of reality and make of it a mere form. Prayer, that is, actual communion with the Living God, is, or should be, the greatest reality judged by effects in us and through us. And yet, have you not at times found yourself on your knees nominally in the act of prayer and yet not conscious of the words you were uttering, still less of the Being to Whom you should be addressing your words? This is not prayer but formality, the great enemy of prayer. David was able to say, "I give myself unto prayer." We have not simply his tongue but his consciousness, his whole attention, his personality, himself, unto this unutterably important spiritual exercise. * **J. R. Mott.**

*From " Anthony Norris Groves " by G. H. Lang, published by the Paternoster Press. by permission

**From " Confronting Young Men with the Living Christ " by J. R. Mott. (London: Hodder & Stoughton).

Make connection before speaking

And there I will meet with thee, and I will commune with thee. Exodus 25 : 22.

Keep silence before me, O islands; and let the people renew their strength : let them come near; then let them speak : let us come near together to judgment. Isa. 41 : 1.

If we would pray aright, the first thing that we should do is to see to it that we really get an audience with God, that we really get into His very presence. Before a word of petition is offered, we should have the definite consciousness that we are talking to God, and should believe that He is listening and is going to grant the thing that we ask of Him. **Dr. R. A. Torrey.**

Remember that you can never be effective for God until you are in communion with God. God's order is communion first, intercession afterward. There may be individual moments when God places a burden on your heart and you go instantly into intercessory warfare, but this is always based upon a life of daily, close communion with the Lord. Apart from guidance otherwise, however, it is good to begin each day with close fellowship with the Lord. Each prolonged prayer time can also begin with such a time of sweet communion. This will include loving adoration of the Lord, and praise and thanksgiving to the Lord. The predominant mood of the Spirit in your soul may and will change from time to time. But none of these elements will long be absent from a life of prayer. **Wesley Duewel.**

And F. B. Meyer gives similar advice : "When the hour for prayer arrives, allow time for staying on the threshold of the temple, to remember how great God is, how greatly He is to be praised, how great your needs are. Remember the distance between you and Him, and be sure that it is filled with love. Recall the promises that bid you to approach. Consider all the holy souls that have entered those same portals; and do not forget the many occasions in which hovering skies have cleared, the dark clouds have parted, and weakness has become power during one brief spell of prayer."

Bless the Lord, O my soul: and all that is within me, bless his holy name. Bless the Lord, O my soul, and forget not all his benefits. **Psa. 103 : 1, 2.**

> What peace! O Gracious Father, God omniscient,
>   Steals o'er the soul this quiet worship hour.
> What wonder fills the mind—as flowing water
>   Fills every crevice—freed from earthly power.
>
> What joy! O precious Lord and tender Saviour,
>   To worship, awed in quiet, prayerful thought;
> When heart and mind forget their selfish purpose
>   And yield to Thee, Whose blood the soul has
>   bought.
>
> What love! O Father, Son and Holy Spirit,
>   Immeasurably outpoured upon the heart.
> O that all time were as this worship hour,
>   Where love and joy and peace would ne'er depart.
>
> **Nettie Chalson**

I do not know a happier employment than to sit down quietly before the Lord and let Him make impressions on your heart— to let Him impress you with His own presence, and to produce whatever influences He will upon you. **E.D.**

And we wish to include the sentiments of the God-controlled missionary, Hudson Taylor:

"The King hath brought me into His chambers. Not first to the banqueting house—that will come in due season; but first to be alone with Himself.

"How perfect! Could we be satisfied to meet a beloved one only in public? No; we want to take such an one aside—to have him all to ourselves. So with our Master: He takes His now fully consecrated bride aside, to taste and enjoy the sacred intimacies of His wondrous love."

Let the King speak NOW

Let my lord the king now speak. II Sam. 14 : 18.

This is my beloved Son, in whom I am well pleased; hear ye him. Matt. 17 : 5.

Are we not apt to think more of speaking to the King than of the King speaking to us? We come to the Throne of Grace with the glad and solemn purpose, "I will now speak unto the King". And we pour out our hearts before Him, and tell Him all the sins and all the needs, all the joys and all the sorrows, till the very telling seems almost an answer, because it brings such a sense of relief. It is very sweet, very comforting to do this.

But this is only half-communion; and we miss, perhaps, a great deal of unknown blessing by being content with this one-sided audience.

We should use another "now", and say, "Let my lord the king now speak". We expect Him to speak some time, but not actually and literally "now", while we kneel before Him. And therefore we do not listen, and therefore we do not hear what He has to say to us.

What about the last time we knelt in prayer? Surely He had more to say to us than we had to say to Him, and yet we never waited a minute to see! We did not give Him opportunity for His gracious response. We rushed away from our King's presence as soon as we had said our say, and vaguely expected Him to send His answers after us somehow and some time, but not there and then. What wonder if they have not yet reached us! The only wonder is that He ever speaks at all when we act thus. If Mary had talked to the Lord Jesus all the time she sat at His feet, she would not have "heard His word". But is not this pretty much what we have done?

Not that we should pray less, but listen more. And the more

we listen, the more we shall want to say afterwards, "Thou shalt call, and I will answer". But we may miss the sweetest whispers of His love by not saying, "Speak, Lord", and not hushing ourselves to "**hear** what God the Lord will speak". We cannot hear His "still, small voice" during a torrent of noisy, and impatient, and hurried petition. "I will watch to see what He will say unto me."

We must "let the King now speak"; not our own hearts and our wandering thoughts, not the world and not the tempter— we must not **let** these speak; they must be silenced with holy determination. And we must let the King speak **as** King, meeting His utterance with implicit submission and faith and obedience; receiving His least hint with total homage, and love, and gratitude.

He has many a blessed surprise for us in thus listening. We may come very diffidently, saying, "Let thine handmaid, I pray thee, speak **one word** unto my lord the King," and having said it, **wait,** saying, "Let my lord the King **now** speak," and then find that He has many **things** to say "to us." **F. R. Havergal.**

John Stam, a young martyr missionary in China, exultingly exclaims : "Take away anything I have, but do not take away the sweetness of walking and talking with the King of Glory ! It is good to let our thoughts run away with us sometimes, concerning the greatness of our God and His marvellous kindness to us. As we look back, what wonderful leadings and providences we see; what encouragement we find for the future."

> Go ! wait before Him where His voice may reach thee.
> Wait where His touch may thrill thee through and through—
> Until His glorious face shall shine upon thee;
> With grace and love undreamed of hitherto.
>
> Forget the busy hours that lie before thee;
> Forget awhile the world of toil and care;
> Forget that other hearts await thy coming;
> Let God Himself alone possess thee there.
>
> **E. H. Divall**

A pause needed

Come ye apart . . . and rest a while. Mark 6 : 31.

And God rested on the seventh day from all his work. Gen. 2 : 2.

There remaineth therefore a rest to the people of God. Heb. 4 : 9.

Dr. X. was telling us some of the fresh wonders of the gramme of radium that America presented to Madame Curie. It is kept buried in a leaden box within two or three other safes, and it needs no direct contact for the doing of its marvellous works. But the marvellous thing is that it cannot keep on giving out all the time. There are periods when it has to be allowed to rest in its quietness and darkness, gathering back, mysteriously, its powers till it can breathe them forth. **Lilias Trotter.**

A gentleman was asked by an artist friend of some note to come to his home, and see a painting just finished. He went at the time appointed, was shown by the attendant into a room which was quite dark, and left there. He was much surprised, but quietly awaited developments. After perhaps fifteen minutes his friend came into the room with a cordial greeting, and took him up to the studio to see the painting, which was greatly admired. Before he left the artist said laughingly, "I suppose you thought it queer to be left in that dark room so long." "Yes," the visitor said, "I did." "Well," his friend replied, "I knew that if you came into my studio with the glare of the street in your eyes you could not appreciate the fine colouring of the picture. So I left you in the dark room till the glare had worn out of your eyes."

Be still and know that God is within thee and around. In the hush of the soul the unseen becomes visible and the eternal real. The eye dazzled by the sun cannot detect the beauties of its perihelion till it has had time to rid itself of the glare. Let

no day pass without its season of silent waiting before God.
F. B. Meyer.

The secret of spiritual power is in being alone with God.
Elijah's victory on Mount Carmel was preceded by his solitude.
Jesus Himself must be much alone with the Father, that He
might speak as never man spoke. If more people had Bunyan's
jail experience, there would be more books like "Pilgrim's
Progress" that would make devils shake and quake and run,
and that would lead people into the experience of salvation.
It was on lonely Patmos, in the silence that could be felt, that
John heard the great voice, and received the messages which
have thrilled God's people in all ages. **M. W. Knapp.**

Alexander Maclaren, looking back on his life, thanks God for
the quiet and obscurity of his early days. "I thank God," he
said once at a public breakfast, "that I was stuck down in a
quiet little obscure place to begin my ministry, for that is what
spoils half of you young fellows, you get pitchforked into
prominent positions at once, and then fritter yourselves away
in all manner of little engagements that you call duties, going
to this tea-meeting, and that anniversary and other breakfast
celebrations, instead of stopping at home and reading your
Bibles and getting near to God. I thank God for the early days
of struggle and obscurity.

"You can crowd Him out of your minds by plunging yourselves
fiercely into your daily duties, however sacred and elevated
these may be. No more than the sunshine can be flashed back
from a tarnished steel mirror, can the consciousness of God's
presence live in an impure soul. And the heart must be kept
still, free from agitation, from the storms of passion and the
tyranny of eager desires. A cat's paw that ruffles the surface
of the lake shatters the image; and unless our hearts are
quieted from earth they will never mirror Heaven."

Fill up the chinks

Blessed is the man that heareth me, watching daily at my gates, waiting at the posts of my doors. Prov. 8 : 34.

Thou wilt keep him in perfect peace, whose mind is stayed on thee. Isa. 26 : 3.

A devotional hour is vital for spiritual vigour, but it is insufficient. All the day through, in the chinks of time, there must be an atmosphere of prayer in which the soul lives.

A traveller hurrying down the road is often chafed by the delay caused by a stop sign or a red signal light as he approaches an intersection. What is to be done with that idle moment ? Let him fill it with prayer. His own soul will be refreshed, and some weary, tempted Christian may receive renewed strength to carry on in the hard battle which is his.

There are so many moments that are lost in the daily performance of our duties. By carefully utilising those moments with prayer we may change the course of many a soul. One great saint of an earlier age affirmed that he never used a blotter in letter writing. Instead, while the ink dried, he would simply close his eyes and offer a prayer for the one to whom he had written.

When one is compelled to wait at the corner for the overdue bus, or in the railroad depot for a delayed train, let him form the habit of praying for the many who are near despair because of frustrated hopes, or cherished plans that did not materialise. Perhaps someone is late to a business appointment and the minutes drag slowly by. Let the one who is compelled to wait use that time to pray. The atmosphere will be more wholesome and friendly when the delayed one finally arrives.

Is there work to be done ? Then go at it bravely and in the spirit of prayer. Let the machinist, as he grinds and polishes the steel, ask God to grind and polish his soul. As the housewife sweeps and dusts her home, let her pray that the

Spirit will sweep from her soul all the things that are not Christ-like. Let the filing clerk pray that a clean record shall be kept in the books of eternity. Thus in every walk of life, while the mind and hands are occupied with common duties, let the soul be in the spirit of prayer.

In the little chinks of time between duties, let the soul turn to God in praise and petition. Make prayer a habit if you would climb the heights of spiritual greatness. **O. G. Wilson.**

"Certain thoughts alone," said Victor Hugo, "are prayers. There are moments, when, whatever the attitude of the body, the soul is on its knees." Another has said, "Our need of prayer is as frequent as the moments of the day; and as we grow in spirituality of mind, our continual need will be felt by us more and more."

> With us no melancholy void,
> No period lingers unemployed
>   Or unimproved, below;
> Our weariness of life is gone,
> Who live to serve our God alone,
>   And only Thee to know.
>
> **Charles Wesley**

May God grant us grace to commune constantly with Himself. Prayer should not be a matter of mornings and evenings alone, but all the day our spirit should commune with God. Father, Thou art so near us, and yet how slow we are to speak to Thee. Teach us thy children, to be always talking with Thee, so that while we walk on earth our conversation may be in Heaven. The Lord give us to hold holy commerce with Heaven, hearing what God the Lord will speak, and speaking to Him in return . . . Perpetual communion with God is the highest state of joy which can be known on earth. Learn to say truthfully, "I have set the Lord always before me", and you have the Lord's secret. **C. H. Spurgeon.**

Hush my heart
to listen

Give ye ear, and hear my voice; hearken, and hear my speech. Isa. 28 : 23.

Blessed are your ears, for they hear. Matt. 13 : 16.

Let us labour therefore to enter into that rest. Heb. 4 : 11.

There is great power in stillness. Sometimes God cannot work through us and for us because of our feverish self-activity. "In quietness and in confidence shall be your strength."

A man who operated an ice house in the old days once lost a gold watch in the sawdust. He offered a reward, and though men went through the sawdust with rakes they were not able to find it. When they left the building for lunch, a small boy went into the ice house and came out a few minutes later with the watch. They asked him how he had found it, and he replied, "I just lay down in the sawdust, and listened, and finally I heard the watch ticking."

There are some of you who have lost more than a watch. If you will be very still and listen quietly, the Lord will speak to you and show you just where you lost the power and the victory which you so sorely miss. Then you will find it again— it will be through the Lord Jesus Christ—as He shows you how sin came and interfered, and how you can get back into fellowship and peace (I John 1). **Redemption Tidings.**

"And he went and lay down. And the Lord called yet again, Samuel" (I Sam. 3 : 5, 6).

God is quiet, He does not make a noise; therefore to understand Him we must be quiet . . . In the hurry and rush of life God is silent; we have to sit at Christ's feet if we would feel His blessing, and then Heaven will be in our heart . . . Before Pentecost the Apostles had to wait ten days . . .

To receive great blessing from the Holy Ghost there must be great preparation.

Philosophers have found that they can think better when they are quiet. How much more then must this be true of the deeper spiritual things ! But those who have had no experience think the desire for quiet is merely laziness. **Sadhu Sundar Singh.**

"Be all at rest"—for rest is highest service;
To the still heart God doth His secrets tell :
Thus shalt thou learn to wait and watch and labour.
Strengthened to bear, since Christ in thee doth dwell.
For what is service but the life of Jesus
Lived through a vessel of earth's fragile clay;
Loving and giving; poured forth for others;
"A living sacrifice" from day to day ?

Freda Hanbury Allen

If you take my advice you will try to get a certain amount of time alone with yourself. I think when we are alone we sometimes see things a little bit more simply, more as they are. Sometimes when we are with others, especially when we are talking to others on religious subjects, we persuade ourselves that we believe more than we do. We talk a great deal, we get enthusiastic, we speak of religious emotions and experiences. This is, perhaps, sometimes good. But when we are alone we just see how much we really believe, how much is mere enthusiasm excited at the moment. We get face to face with Him and our heat and passion go, and what is really permanent remains. We begin to recognise how very little love we have, how very little real pleasure in that which is alone of lasting importance. Then we see how poor and hollow and unloving we are; then, I think we also begin to see that this poverty, this hollowness, this unloving void can only be filled by Him who fills all in all. To get alone—to dare to be alone—with God, this, I am persuaded, is one of the best ways of doing anything in the world. It is possible to be constantly speaking of Him, to glow with enthusiasm as we talk about Him to others, and yet to be half-conscious that we dare not quietly face Him alone. **F. Robinson.**

Guard the interior life

Man looketh on the outward appearance, but the Lord looketh on the heart. I Sam. 16 : 7.

Do ye look on things after the outward appearance? II Cor. 10 : 7.

The rightly rounded Christian life has two sides; the **out**-side, and the **inner**-side. To most of us the outer side seems the greater. The living, the serving, the giving, the doing, the absorption in life's work, the contact with men, with the great majority the sheer struggle for existence—these take the greater thought and time of us all. They seem to be the great business of life even to those of us who thoroughly believe in the inner life.

But when the real eyes open, the inner eyes that see the unseen, the change of perspective is first ludicrous, then terrific, then pathetic. Ludicrous, because of the change of proportions; terrific, because of the issues at stake; pathetic, because of strong men that see not, and push on spending splendid strength whittling sticks. The outer side is narrow in its limits. It has to do with food and clothing, bricks and lumber, time and the passing hour, the culture of the mind, the joys of social contact, the smoothing of the way for the suffering. And it needs not to be said, that these are right; they belong in the picture; they are its physical background.

The inner side includes all of these, and stretches infinitely beyond. Its limits are broad; broad as the home of man; with its enswathing atmosphere added. It touches the inner spirit. It moves in upon the motives, the loves, the heart. It moves out upon the myriad spirit-beings and forces that swarm ceaselessly about the earth staining and sliming men's souls and lives. It moves up to the arm of God in co-operation with His great love-plan for a world. **S. D. Gordon.**

We love to spread our branches
   The root-life we neglect;
We love to shine in public,
   And human praise expect;
While in the inner chamber
   Where creature voices cease,
We may meet God in silence
   And breathe in heaven's peace.
The secret of deep living
   Lies in the secret place,
Where, time and sense forgotten,
   We see God face to face;
Beyond mere forms and symbols,
   Beyond mere words and signs,
Where in that hidden temple
   The light eternal shines.

Max I. Reich

Never were men more tempted to live their lives in the outer courts of things, and neglect or forget the central shrine, the habitation of sovereignty and holiness and peace. We are tempted to live in the show of things, and not in the heart of things themselves. We are tempted to build a house of incidents, and omit the essentials. Am I not transcribing the modern temperament, the modern peril, and the modern experience ? Is it not true that our danger is to prize the husk and throw away the kernel, to emphasise the living more than the life, to pass our days in the streets of existence, and miss the mysterious, deepening glory of its innermost room ? The snare of today is the neglect of the secret place.
Dr. J. H. Jowett.

Prayer's quiet retreat on a busy day

And he took him aside from the multitude. Mark 7 : 33.

And Peter put them all forth, and kneeled down, and prayed. Acts 9 : 40.

This is not a praying age. Every call is to work, to activity. We are living in most strenuous times. The pressure of active duty is tremendous. In all departments of life this is true. Men have little time for leisure. In the church, too, the call is to activity. The cry is for the evangelising of the world. It is a missionary age in which we are living. Christians hear but little about the duty of meditation, of devotion, of prayer—they are called rather out into the field to work, to hasten the coming of the kingdom.

This is well. Every redeemed life should be consecrated to service. But there is danger in this intense activity. The danger is not that we become too strenuous in carrying the Gospel to men—this never could be—but that we get too little quiet in our lives for the cultivations of our own heart piety. There must be root before there can be strong branches and much fruit. We must sit at Christ's feet to be fed before we can go out to feed others. Not a word should be said to restrain earnestness, to check enthusiasm in Christ's work, to hold anyone back from the service of Christ. But in our much serving and work we should never forget the necessity of Bible reading and communion with Christ, to prepare us for the noble work we are striving to do. All the best things of Christian life are the fruit of silent meditation.

Life is not easy for any of us. We can live grandly, purely, Christianly only by being much with Christ. We will rob ourselves of Divine blessing, of beauty of character, of power in service, if we fail to make room in all our busy days for quiet retreats from noise and strife, where we may sit at

Christ's feet to hear His words, and lie on His bosom that we may absorb His spirit, to prepare us for the toil and the witnessing. **J. R. Miller.**

"Let not your works of mercy," said John Wesley, "rob you of time for private prayer." And in a letter to a friend, he writes: "I find the engaging, though but a little, in these temporal affairs is apt to dampen and deaden the soul; and there is no remedy but continual prayer. What, then, but the mighty power of God can keep your soul alive, who are engaged all the day long in such a multiplicity of them? It is well that His grace is sufficient for you. But do you not find need to pray always? And if you can't always say,

> 'My hands are but employed below,
> My heart is still with Thee",

is there not the more occasion for some season of solemn retirement (if it were possible, every day), wherein you may withdraw your mind from earth, and even the accounts between God and your own soul?"

> Sometimes I have so much to do
> I think it must be done.
> I'll work so very, very hard
> From morn till set of sun,
> But here is something I have found;
> This really doesn't pay.
> I've always found I've weaker grown
> If I have failed to pray.
>
> So I am trying hard to learn
> That nothing's really great
> If I must take my praying time,
> So praying has to wait.
> It's praying makes me fit to work;
> It is my staff and stay,
> And work will never be my best,
> If I have failed to pray.

Selected

Two ways
of praying

And Jacob was left alone; and there wrestled a man with him until the breaking of the day. Gen. 32 : 24.

And being in an agony he prayed more earnestly : and his sweat was as it were great drops of blood falling down to the ground. Luke 22 : 44.

There are two ways of praying. One asks and hopes; the other craves and waits until he has obtained. It is just this "until" that characterises the latter.

One seeks God and finds Him; the other strives with God and triumphs. The first observes scrupulously his daily devotions; the second stays on his knees hours a day, through the night.

The first fits in with the ordinary course of life; the second watches, fasts, cries, weeps, sweats blood.

The first is the beaten path below, winding in the plain; the second is the hard way of the perfect, scaling rock, sounding the depth, grazing the precipice's edge.

The first is the irreproachable method of brother or sister so-and-so; the second is that of Jacob at Peniel, of Moses on Sinai, of Elijah on Carmel, of Jesus in the wilderness, in Gethsemane, on Golgotha.

The first we have known since we learned to know the Lord; the second . . . Lord teach us to pray !

"Men ought always to pray and not to faint." But how hard, when fainting, to pray ! I profited by my railway journey to Nimes to pray. I would wish to work less and to pray more. But to work, read, write, speak—all this is easier than to pray. May He Who changed the water to wine make of a rheumatic, discouraged, uncertain, suffering one all that he ought to be to glorify Him by a faithful testimony. **M. Monod.**

None of us need look for illustrations of the first kind of prayer. They are all too familiar. We find this second type of praying to have been the secret behind the godly men and women of all times, whether they were ministers, tradesmen or praying mothers. The cost of a Spirit-owned ministry is shown by a brief statement by Harold St. John that impressed us much.

"A sleepless night, but I got my sermon on the floor between three and four in the morning. Preaching is a happy labour but I must give blood every time. A fearful month's work lies ahead and I must pray a great deal. I am clumsy, unaccustomed to His easy yoke. Jacob's lesson must still be mine—he prevailed. Will He give me what I want—power with the angel ?"

Flavel observed : "To shuffle over religious duties with a loose and heedless spirit will cost no great pains; but to set thyself before the Lord and to tie up thy loose ends and vain thoughts to constant and serious attendance upon Him—this will cost thee something."

Jeremy Taylor says, "Easiness of desire is a great enemy to the success of a good man's prayer. It must be an intent, zealous, busy, operative prayer; for, consider what a huge indecency it is that a man should speak to God for a thing that he values not ! Our prayers upbraid our spirits when we beg tamely for those things for which we ought to die, which are more precious than imperial sceptres, richer than the spoils of the sea, or the treasures of the Indian hills."

A Christian can obtain deep feeling, by thinking on the object. God is not going to pour these things on you, without any effort of your own. You must cherish the slightest impressions. Take the Bible, and go over the passages that show the condition and prospects of the world. Look at the world, look at your children, and your neighbours and see their condition while they remain in sin, and persevere in prayer and effort till you obtain the blessing of the Spirit of God to dwell in you. **C. Finney.**

Pray according to his will

I exhort therefore, that, first of all, supplications, prayers, intercessions, and giving of thanks, be made for all men . . . for this is good and acceptable in the sight of God our Saviour who will have all men to be saved, and to come unto the knowledge of the truth. I Tim. 2:1, 3, 4.

That ye might be filled with the knowledge of his will. Col. 1:9.

In the New Testament two Greek words are used for **intercession,** the one meaning to fall in with the desire of another, the other to devise a plan to meet a need. (See I Tim. 2:1; Rom. 8:24, 27).

The intercessor, in an audience with God, discovers His plan, and, falling in with His will, becomes the channel through which there is carried out the divine purpose. There is suggested in this meaning of intercession a side to prayer of infinite value, but which may not always be present to the mind of a believer.

In the life and service to which a Christian is called it is a matter of the utmost importance for him to acquire the habit of instant reference to God through prayer of every matter of concern. To emphasise this is not unnecessary, because the natural disposition of each of us is to deal with a difficulty, or a need, **first of all on human lines.** We form our own plans and have much cause in the future for regret. We hasten to take counsel of others, with the frequent experience that advice, given wholly by the intellect, leads to no real and permanent result; so finding our difficulties increased.

Intercession, to reach its end, must look at the needs of the world or the Church from the standpoint of Calvary, for the important factor in prayer is not the sense of human need, but the discovery of the plan of God, while the condition of answered prayer is coinciding with His will. Here is the truth which brings help and gives light—"Likewise also the Spirit helpeth our infirmities . . . the Spirit Himself maketh intercession for us." **G. B. Watt.**

Amy Carmichael, founder of the Dohnavur Fellowship, writing of their experiences said, "One of the earliest lessons we learned together was that before asking for anything, we should find out if it were according to the mind of the Lord. This kind of prayer needed time—time to listen, to understand, to **wait.** The more we pondered over all the Bible says about prayer, the more we found to make us ask to be **filled with the knowledge of His will** before offering petitions for a desired good." Hudson Taylor encouraged this kind of waiting: "Better," he said, "to wait on God before commencing a project, than to hurry into some self-inspired endeavour and **then** to ask God's blessing on it."

"And this is the boldness which we have toward him," says St. John in I John 5:14, "That, if we ask anything according to His will, He heareth us: and if we know that He heareth us whatsoever we ask, we know that we have the petitions which we have asked of Him."

> Toiling in rowing I have done today
>   When I should have waited on Him
> Who is the Captain of all of life's way.
>   He knows when the prospects are dim,
> And will tell me in time where to cast the net
>   For the draught he would have me bring;
> He never has failed a trusting child yet . . .
>   They obey, then let their hearts sing!
> Lord, no more toiling in rowing . . .
> I'll fling my net where'er You direct,
>   Whatever Your purpose for me;
> My will and ambitions, all my plans, I subject
>   For guidance, dear Lord, unto Thee!

Jessie Whiteside Finks

Helpers together in prayer

Praying also for us, that God would open unto us a door of utterance, to speak the mystery of Christ. Col. 4 : 3.

Strive together with me in your prayers to God for me. Rom. 15 : 30.

Finally, brethren, pray for us, that the word of the Lord may have free course, and be glorified. II Thess. 3 : 1.

Intercession should be definite and detailed. Vagueness is lifelessness. St. Paul besought the Romans to pray for him, and then told them exactly what he wanted, four definite petitions to be presented for him. It is a help to reality of intercession when ministers or other workers who ask our prayers will tell us exactly what they want. General prayers for "blessing" are apt to become formal.

We must not yield to the idea that, because we are feeble members, doing no great work, our prayers "won't make much difference". It may be that this is the very reason why the Lord keeps us in the shade, because He hath need of us (though we feel no better than an "ass's colt") for the work of intercession. Many of us only learn to realise the privilege of being called to this by being called apart from all other work. When this is the case, let us simply and faithfully do it, "lifting up holy hands, without wrath and doubting", blessing His name Who provides this holy and beautiful service for those who "**by night** stand in the house of the Lord".

See how wonderfully St. Paul valued the prayers of others. He distinctly expresses this to every Church but one to whom he wrote. Would he have asked their prayers so fervently if he thought it would not "make much difference"? **F. R. Havergal.**

We evangelists get a lot of credit—and very often take what is not ours at all. A woman in Ireland who prays for hours, prays each day for this poor stammerer. Others tell me, "Never a day passes but what I lay hold of God for you." They have brought to birth many that are credited to me, whereas I very often only act as a midwife. In the judgment we shall be amazed to see big rewards go to unknown disciples. Sometimes I think we preachers who catch the eyes of the public will be among those rewarded the least. **L. Ravenhill.**

Mrs. Howard Taylor in her book, "Pastor Hsi", reveals who was the secret prayer-helper behind the scenes who prevailed with God :

"But was it David Hill who won Hsi to Christ ? Or was it he alone ? Long after both were gone, the writer received the following letter, penned by one of his colleagues at Hankow :

" 'May I give you an unpublished incident, told me by Mr. Hill himself. Mr. Hill had a dear friend in England, who was distinguished for her power in prayer. When she died, an unfinished letter was found upon her desk intended for Mr. Hill, and was forwarded to him by the family. In it this lady told Mr. Hill how she had recently been much drawn out in prayer on his behalf, and had specially been led to plead for an extraordinary blessing to be given to him in his work at that time. She felt distinctly that she had been heard, though she knew not what form the blessing would take. The date of this letter was found so closely to correspond with the conversion of Pastor Hsi, that Mr. Hill never doubted but that that was the extraordinary blessing given in answer to his friend's prayer.' "

> Stir me ! oh stir me, Lord. Thy heart was stirred
> By love's intensest fire, 'til Thou didst give
> Thine only Son, Thy best beloved One,
> E'en to the dreadful cross, that I might live.
> Stir me to give myself so back to Thee
> That Thou canst give Thyself again, through me.
>
> **Mrs. A. Head**

When prayer is a cry

Hezekiah the king, and the prophet Isaiah . . . prayed and cried to heaven. And the Lord sent an angel. II Chron. 32 : 20, 21.

When they returned, and cried unto thee, thou heardest them from heaven; and many times didst thou deliver them according to thy mercies. Neh. 9 : 28.

And she was in bitterness of soul, and prayed unto the Lord, and wept sore. I Sam. 1 : 10.

God can hear a whispered prayer, but He does not often answer it. If prayer were simply confidential "love talk", a whisper would often suffice. But when prayer becomes supplication, nothing can substitute for a cry.

When men care enough to cry, God heeds their request and answers their prayer. Crying suggests earnestness. According to the proverb, the pursuit of wisdom is not easy : "If thou criest after knowledge, and liftest up thy voice for understanding; if thou seekest her as silver, and searchest for her as for hid treasures; then shalt thou . . . find the wisdom of God" (Prov. 2 : 3-5). To be earnest is to be wholehearted. It is to aim at the one goal which, if one misses, he loses everything.

Crying suggests desperation. Only a desperate religion is real. I use the word "desperate" in the sense of staking one's whole life and happiness upon it. If religion is a hobby or a sideline, it cannot be desperate or real.

Desperate (not, frantic) men are not necessarily good, but good men dare not play it "cool". Good men realise that their all is at stake in God. "Whom have I in heaven but thee ? and there is none upon earth that I desire beside thee" (Psalm 73 : 25).

In the days of His flesh our Lord Himself "offered up prayers and supplications with strong crying and tears unto him that was able to save him . . . and was heard". Jesus did not consider prayer as mere polite conversation with His Father. A divine work was to be accomplished in Jesus' earth mission, and it could not be accomplished without groans, tears, and a cross.

Why do we not cry unto God ? Are our desires too weak ?
Are we ashamed to seem desperate ? There's a sob in the
heart of God, and the eyes of men around the world flow with
tears, tears which arise because of broken hearts, empty
dreams, futile quests, unfulfilled hopes. Earth has no balm for
the wounds of men. Satan can tease man's mind but he cannot
rest man's heart.

Only those that weep can reach that land beyond tears. And
only those who go forth weeping, bearing precious seed, will
come to glory with rejoicing, bringing their sheaves with them.
G. E. Failing.

Great grief prays with great earnestness. There are sorrows
that make men real. There are paroxysms of the soul that
drive men mad. Under the pressure of grief the balance is lost,
but such madness is not lunacy; it is the sublimest reason.
There are prayers that are cold and correct, decorous and
formal, but they work no miracles.

Prayer is not a collection of balanced phrases; it is the
pouring out of the soul. What is love if it be not fiery ? What
are prayers if the heart be not ablaze ? They are the battles of
the soul. In them men wrestle with principalities and powers . . .

The prayer that prevails is not the work of lips and
fingertips. It is the cry of a broken heart and the travail of a
stricken soul. Of Jesus it is said, "As he prayed, he sweat".
He never sweat over the wonders He wrought, but praying
brought the sweat of blood. *****Samuel Chadwick.**

> Stir me ! oh stir, Lord, 'til prayer is pain—
> 'Til prayer is joy—'til prayer turns into praise !
> Stir me, 'til heart and will and mind—yes all
> Is wholly Thine to use through all the days.
> Stir, 'til I learn to pray exceedingly,
> Stir, 'til I learn to wait expectantly.

Mrs. A. Head

*From The Path of Prayer by Samuel Chadwick. (London : Hodder & Stoughton).
Copyright 1931 by Samuel Chadwick. Copyright 1956 Hodder & Stoughton Limited.

Prayer
and revival

**All this evil is come upon us: yet made we not our prayer
before the Lord our God, that we might turn from our
iniquities, and understand thy truth. Dan. 9:13.**

**Now therefore, O our God, hear the prayer of thy servant, and
his supplications, and cause thy face to shine upon thy
sanctuary that is desolate, for the Lord's sake. Dan. 9:17.**

Usually when God intends greatly to bless a church, it will
begin in this way—two or three persons in it are distressed at
the low state of affairs and become troubled even to anguish.

Perhaps they do not know of their common grief but they
begin to pray with flaming desire and untiring importunity. The
passion to see the church revived rules them. They think of it
as they go to rest. They dream of it on their bed. They muse
on it in the streets. This one thing consumes them. They
suffer great heaviness and continual sorrow in heart for
perishing sinners. They travail in birth for souls.

Lord, give me a dozen importunate pleaders and lovers of
souls, and by Thy grace I will shake London from end to end.

God's work would go on without the mass of you Christians.
Many of you only hinder the march of God's army. But give us
a dozen lion-like, lamb-like men burning with intense love to
Christ and souls, and nothing will be impossible to their faith.

Who are they that hinder? I answer. Every worldly Christian
hinders the progress of the Gospel. Every member of a church
who is living in secret sin, who is tolerating in his heart
anything he knows is wrong, who is not seeking eagerly his
own personal sanctification, is to that extent—hindering the
work of the Spirit.

Be ye clean, ye that bear the vessels of the Lord, for to the
extent that we maintain known unholiness, we restrain the
Spirit. He cannot work among us as long as any conscious sin
is tolerated.

It is not overt breaking of Commandments I am speaking of
but I include worldliness also—a care for carnal things and a

carlessness about spiritual things : having enough grace to make us hope you are a Christian but not enough to prove you are; bearing a shrivelled apple here and there on the topmost bough, but not much fruit; this I mean—this partial barrenness, not complete enough to condemn, yet complete enough to restrain the blessing—this hinders revival and the progress of the Church.

Some of you Christians do not put your hand to pull. Then the rest of us have to labour so much the more, and the worst of it is we have to draw you also. While you do not add to the strength that draws, you increase the weight that is to be drawn.

Oh, by the wounds and bloody sweat of the Saviour, I beseech you, followers of Christ, be in earnest—that the Name of the Lord may be known and loved among men through your life and earnest testimony and the agonising endeavours of the Christian Church. **C. H. Spurgeon.**

I feel more and more deeply, every time I address meetings, that you may have an earnest Christian, a godly man or woman, and yet his or her life be far below what God could make it, if he or she would wait for the Holy Spirit to get possession. Believers, I want to call you to be intercessors, I want to plead with you by the needs of London with its millions of people, by the needs of heathenism with its hundreds of millions, and by the needs of the Church of Christ, alas ! alas ! with its multitudes of nominal professors and half-hearted Christians—will you not be intercessors ? Will you not give up yourselves to walk in the footsteps of Christ, and to become fountains of blessing to this weary world ? Oh, come and let the Holy Ghost have you entirely today, and then He will teach you how to pray. **Andrew Murray.**

Praying
for our enemies

Pray for them which despitefully use you. Matt. 5 : 44.

Forgive us our sins; for we also forgive everyone. Luke 11 : 4.

I am convinced we have far too shallow views of that command
to pray for our enemies. It means a vast more than to say,
"God bless our foes". It means that we are to take them on
our heart in good earnest, and intercede for them,
particularly, lovingly, perseveringly—pray for them—till out of
a loving heart we can unite their highest welfare with our own.

I have been blessed all my life with a few enemies; at a few
periods in my life with a great many, and sometimes they have
been exceedingly bitter. But in reviewing the past, I notice that
I have had the fewest enemies and the most popularity when I
was the least spiritual and the farthest away from God. And
when I have had deepest fellowship with Christ, I have been
the most misunderstood by religious people, and the most
intensely hated by bad people.

I can recall many seasons when I felt it a necessity to pray
especially both for positive enemies and for Christian people
who had greatly injured me, while they did not intend to be
my foes. A certain very bitter enemy had done many things to
greatly damage both me and my family. I had often prayed for
him in my secret devotions, but one day I felt drawn to go off
alone into a forest and spend some hours in pleading to God
for him and his family.

At the beginning of my prayer, I tried to exercise great
charity for the man by putting myself in his place, and looking
at my own miserable self from his standpoint. But the Spirit
soon showed me that was the human way, and not the divine.
It came to me that what I needed was to love that man with
the identical same love that Jesus had for him; to pity,

sympathise with, and feel toward him exactly as God felt, up to my capacity; that I was to be a living vessel in such union with the Holy Spirit—that Jesus could love him through me, and pour His divine love through my affections.

It was revealed to me that in order to love him as Christ loved I must utterly abandon my being to the Holy Spirit, for the purpose of becoming a channel of the perfectly unselfish, impartial, disinterested, tender, and boundless compassion of God.

I complied with the suggestion of the Spirit, and before I had prayed an hour the fountains of my soul were broken up, my tears flowed like rain; all his welfare of body and soul, all his family, all his temporal and eternal interests, became very precious in my sight.

As I continued to plead with God for his soul's salvation, and for all his welfare in detail, suddenly the Spirit opened to my mind what a lovely Christian that man would make if he were thoroughly washed in Jesus' blood, and filled with the Holy Spirit. I seemed to see his soul and all his gifts and powers, now so perverted by sin—how lovely they would be if transformed by divine grace! As I viewed him under the possibilities of saving grace, he seemed transfigured in my vision.

I then prayed that I might feel a Christlike grief for any trouble that might befall him. From that moment it has been easy and sweet to pray for him, and I never think of him except with a peculiarly tender love.

Not only must we pray long and fervently for our positive foes, but pray much for religious people who are cold and severe to us; for if we do not keep our hearts warm and pure, and very tender to everybody on earth, we lose that sweet sense of oneness with Jesus which is worth more than all the friendship of creatures. It is not my calling to make people love me; it is my great business to have perfect union with the Holy Spirit, and to love all with God's love, whether they love or have confidence in me or not. **George D. Watson.**

Praying
for God

Prayer also shall be made for him continually; and daily shall he be praised. Psa. 72 : 15.

Hallowed be thy name. Matt. 6 : 9.

Not unto us, O Lord, not unto us, but unto thy name give glory. Psa. 115 : 1.

Prayer for Him! Prayer for the welfare of Christ! The words are startling, the sentiment more startling still. I have been accustomed to pray for those in need—for the poor, the squalid, the vicious. But to pray for God, to supplicate in behalf of a Being Who is exalted above all other beings—is not that a profane thing! No, my brother; it is very holy—the most pious of all prayers.

When you say that your Christ is exalted above all other beings, did it never strike you that you have declared Him to be in need! To be exalted above all things is for Divine Love a source of deepest pain. The pain of Divine Love is just this elevation—this eminence, alone. It longs to step down, to break its solitude. It longs to behold in humanity a mirror of itself—another self whom it can speak to.

Did you ever ask yourself why in teaching men to pray our Lord told them to pray first for the Father? Why did He bid them begin by saying, "Hallowed be Thy name, Thy kingdom come, Thy will be done"? Was not **our** need of daily bread more pressing? No. Christ knew that there was no hunger equal to the hunger of the Father. He knew that the heart of Divine Love was famished . . . He bids us remember the **Divine** want ere we remember the human . . . Think of the Father's loneliness, think of the Father's prayer! Remember Love's poverty **without** love! Remember the solitude of a God without communion! Let **Him** have your first sympathy, your earnest prayer!

O Thou Who hast taken into Thy hand the work of the Father, I shall pray continually for Thee! I often pray **to** Thee:

I shall learn to pray **for** Thee. I have been taught from my childhood to say "for Christ's sake", "for Jesus' sake", but I did not realise its meaning. I never understood that I was asking for Thy **joy** . . . Whatever I ask, let it be for **Thy** sake! If I desire gold, let it be for Thy manger! If I desire the gift of song, let it be for Thy Bethlehem! If I desire the hour of mirth, let it be for Thy Cana! If I desire the joys of home, let it be for Thy Nazareth! Let me treasure the alabaster for **Thee,** the spices for Thee! If I ask wealth, let it be to feed Thy poor! If I ask health, let it be to bear Thy journeys! If I ask eloquence, let it be to repeat Thine accents! If I ask beauty, let it be to reflect Thine image! If I ask the strength of a resurrection body, let it be to help Thy burden! So shall my supplications be songs of love; my prayers will all be praises when they are prayers for Thee. **G. Matheson.**

> Not watch one hour? He said,
> In garden of His pain,
> Fruitless His plaint, the flesh was faint,
> They sighed, and slept again.
>
> So to our slothful souls
> Steals thy sad patient plea,
> **I live for you, O friends untrue,**
> **Have ye no care for me?**
>
> **Joseph Truman**

It is God's "delight . . . to be with the children of men". His heart is not isolated and unfeeling, but full of the spirit of communication. He not only loves but loves to be loved. The desire of His heart is not, and cannot be satisfied until man not only returns to be reconciled, but returns with the full purpose never more to be un-reconciled; in other words, returns to **live** in Him. **Thomas C. Upham.**

Prayer
for our loved ones

For this child I prayed; and the Lord hath given me my petition which I asked of him : therefore also I have lent him to the Lord; as long as he liveth he shall be lent to the Lord. I Sam. 1 : 27, 28.

Job . . . rose up early in the morning, and offered burnt offerings according to the number of them all (his sons and daughters) . . . Thus did Job continually. Job 1 : 5.

I have at times been asked by some earnest, sensitive persons if it is not selfish to be especially concerned for one's own, over whom the heart yearns much, and the prayer offered is more tender and intense and more frequent. Well, if **you** do not pray for them, who will ? Who **can** pray for them with such believing persistent fervour as you ? God has set us in the relationship of personal affection and of kinship for just such a purpose. He binds us together with the ties of love that we may be concerned for each other. If there be but one in a home in touch with God, that one becomes God's door into the whole family.

Contact means opportunity, and that in turn means responsibility. The closer the contact the greater the opportunity and the greater too the responsibility. Unselfishness does not mean to exclude one's self, and one's own. It means right proportions in our perspective . . . Not only is it not selfish so to pray, it is a part of God's plan that we should so pray. I am most responsible for the one to whom I am most closely related.

Man **is** a free agent, to use the old phrase, so far as God is concerned; utterly, wholly free. And, he is the most enslaved agent on the earth, so far as sin, and selfishness and prejudice are concerned. The purpose of our praying is not to force or coerce his will; never that. It is to free his will of the warping influences that now twist it awry. It is to get the dust out of his eyes so his sight shall be clear. And once he is free, able to see aright, to balance things without prejudice, the whole probability is in favour of his using his will to choose the only right.

I want to suggest to you the ideal prayer for such a one. It is an adaptation of Jesus' own words. It may be pleaded with much variety of detail. It is this: deliver him from the evil one; and work in him Thy will for him, by Thy power to Thy glory in Jesus, the Victor's name. **S. D. Gordon.**

William Carvosso, an early Methodist class-leader, used to spend hours, literally hours, at a time, praying for the conversion of individual persons. His religion was taken into the home, and he prayed the prayer of faith for the conversion of his children. "I had always prayed," he said, "for my children; but now I grasped the promise with the hand of faith, and retired daily at special seasons to put the Lord to His word. I said nothing of what I felt, or did, to anyone but the Searcher of Hearts with Whom I wrestled in an agony of prayer.

"About a fortnight after I had been thus engaged with God, being at work in the field, I received a message from my wife, informing me that I was wanted within." The outcome was that he was able to lead two of his children to Christ almost immediately, and a few days later his other child was converted. In later years he said, "I have often thought, if parents were to plead more importunately with God on behalf of their own offspring, He would surely hear their cry; and we should not see so many professors' children living in a state of ungodliness and sin."

"Your part in intercessory prayer," says Oswald Chambers, "is not to enter into the agony of intercession, but to utilise the commonsense circumstances God puts you in, and the commonsense people He puts you amongst by His providence, to bring them before God's throne and give the Spirit in you a chance to intercede for them. In this way God is going to sweep the whole world with His saints."

Asking on behalf of others

We do not cease to pray for you. Col. 1 : 9.
Pray one for another, that ye may be healed. James 5 : 16.

Whatever other ends are answered by prayer, this is one, and it seems the primary one, that we may have the petitions which we ask of Him. Asking is the appointed means of receiving, and that for others as well as for ourselves; as we may learn partly from reason itself, but more fully from our own experience, and more clearly still from revelation.

Reason teaches us to argue from analogy. If you (because you have a regard for me) would do more for a third person at my request than otherwise you would have done, how much more will God at the request of His beloved children give blessings to those they pray for which otherwise He would not have given !

And how does all experience confirm this ! How many times have the petitions of others been answered to our advantage, and ours on the behalf of others.

But the most decisive of all proofs is the Scripture, "Go to my servant Job, and he shall pray for you; for him I will accept." It was not a temporal blessing which was here in question, but a spiritual, the forgiveness of their sin. So when St. Paul said, "Brethren, pray for us," he did not desire this on a temporal account only, that "he might be delivered out of the mouth of the lion," but on a spiritual, "that he might speak boldly as he ought to speak." But the instances of this are innumerable. In proof of the general truth that God gives us both temporal blessings and spiritual blessings in answer to each other's prayers I need only remind you of one Scripture more : "Let them pray over him; and the prayer of faith shall save the sick; and if he hath committed sins, they shall be forgiven him." The promise in the following verse is still more comprehensive : "Pray one for another, and ye shall be healed" of whatsoever you have confessed to each other. **John Wesley.**

Because you prayed—
God touched our weary bodies with His power
And gave us strength for many a trying hour
In which we might have faltered, had not you,
Our intercessors, faithful been, and true.

Because you prayed—
God touched our lips with coals from altar fire,
Gave Spirit-fullness, and did so inspire
That, when we spoke, sin-blinded souls did see;
Sin's chains were broken;
Captives were made free.

Charles B. Bowser

The promises are not given to our wants, but to our petitions. **Whatleley.**

How hard the people's hearts seem! How immovable! For it is only "when we pray that something gives way", and we find that God has been before us, breaking down the barriers, and softening the hard ground, so preparing it for the seed of His Word, which the great Sower, the Holy Spirit, will implant through us.

"It is evident," says a worker, rejoicing over two souls saved, "that while I have been praying, God has been creating a thirst for Himself in these two hearts, and now He has satisfied it."

One who is anxious about those in her own family says, "When I am more constantly in earnest prayer for them, I notice they seem more desirous of knowing more about Jesus Christ, and to walk with Him, but when I get lax in prayer they seem to fall back into their old spiritual sleepiness."

Prayer is bound to leave its mark on the lives for which we intercede. **Constance Ruspini.**

Pray that they may pray more

Cease not to cry unto the Lord our God for us. I Sam. 7 : 8.

And Samuel cried unto the Lord for Israel; and the Lord heard him. I Sam. 7 : 9.

I know that this shall turn to my salvation through your prayer, and the supply of the Spirit of Jesus Christ. Phil. 1 : 19.

What shall you ask for us in the mission field? What benison, what benediction would you bestow on isolated missionaries through prayers?

There is nothing more profitable, more priceless that you can ask for us, than that in spite of physical weariness, and "often infirmities", and cares of many churches among multiplying converts, we may be enabled to remain upon our knees. For there is a praying in detail that has to be done if the infant churches are to grow and prosper. And that detailed praying can only be done by those on the field. Only we can know the names, the lives, the temptations, of the converts.

"Prayer must ever be primary"; all other service even in the field, is but secondary. But we earnestly desire "through your prayers, and the supply of the Spirit", that we might be given enough spiritual energy to "make full proof" of this most vital ministry.

But we need your help. For "who is sufficient for these things"?

Prayer so wonderfully enriches all other activities. And, "if any will not work, neither shall he eat", is true also of this "work" of prayer. If there is not in our lives that quality of urgency which must find an outlet in the "conflict" of prayer, then neither shall we know the rarest, richest fruits of God, of the Spirit. It is your prayers which can best strengthen us to fulfil this unique service.

Your prayers can make our praying specially cogent and powerful. It is an accepted fact that the effectual preaching of the Gospel owes its convincing effect largely to the concentrated prayers of many saints. So many prayers, focused on a preacher, give his words and preaching ministry a supernatural and extraordinary power, not his own. Yet, though not generally realised, this is even more true of the prayer ministry of the one prayed for. There is a cumulative effect in prayer.

So when you seek God's face for us, above all ask that we may be enabled to pray and to go on praying. You can ask nothing more profitable, more potent. Pray that the Spirit may so store our hearts with blessed urgings, and "groanings which cannot be uttered", that relief must be found in persistent, unwearying prayer. Pray that we may indeed be "straightened" in spirit till this exacting ministry be accomplished. So surely will Christ's church be edified and His coming hastened.
N. Deck.

Did you think of us this morning
As you breathed a word of prayer?
Did you ask for strength to help us
All our heavy burdens bear?
Did you speak of faith and courage
For the trials we must meet?
Did you ask that God might help us
As you bowed at Jesus' feet?
Someone prayed and strength was given
For the long and weary road;
Someone prayed and faith grew stronger
As we bent beneath our load;
Someone prayed—the way grew brighter
And we walked all unafraid—
In our heart a song of gladness—
Tell us, was it you who prayed?

Selected

How to pray for the lost

For the weapons of our warfare are not carnal, but mighty through God to the pulling down of strong holds; casting down imaginations (margin—"reasonings"), and every high thing that exalteth itself against the knowledge of God, and bringing into captivity every thought to the obedience of Christ. (II Cor. 10 : 4, 5).

The author, wishing to remain anonymous, says: This is the result of my search for the right way of praying for the unsaved. I have found it to produce amazing results in a short time . . . I have taken my place of authority in Christ and am using it against the enemy. I have not looked at myself to see if I were fit or not; I've just taken my place and have prayed for the quickening of the Holy Spirit.

Intercession must be persistent, not to persuade God, for redemption is of God, but because of the enemy. Our prayer and resistance are against the enemy, the awful powers and rulers of darkness. It is our duty before God to fight for the souls for whom Christ died. Just as some must preach to them the good news of their redemption, just so others must fight back the powers of darkness on their behalf.

Satan yields only what and when he must, and he renews his attacks in subtle ways. Therefore, prayer must be persisted in, even long after definite results are seen. And we must hold what is taken for God against the enemy until such time as that soul is firmly established in the faith.

We will find that as we pray the Holy Spirit will give new leads. Always follow His leads. We were interceding for a soul recently and felt that our prayers were not making contact. It seemed that there was nothing there. Then the Holy Spirit inspired us to begin to draw them unto God in the name of the Lord Jesus. As we obeyed this leading, repeating "I draw —unto God in the name of the Lord Jesus", we felt our prayers gradually take hold. It seemed that we were drawing that one from deep within the very camp of the enemy. Then we were able to proceed as usual, claiming every detail of that life for God, holding the blood against the enemy. This is true warfare in the spirit realm. Thank God that our spiritual weapons are mighty and that our authority in Christ is far above all the authority of the rulers, the principalities and powers of darkness, so that the enemy is obliged to yield. But it takes faith, patience and persistence.

Missionaries on foreign and home fields can resist the enemy in their districts, communities and schools, by holding the blood of Jesus against the powers of darkness, sin and unbelief, in the authority of the name of Jesus. In the name of the Lord Jesus they can demand that the enemy retreat.

We would like to point out that "it is the Spirit that quickeneth; the flesh profiteth nothing". "The letter killeth, but the Spirit giveth life." Therefore, we must constantly seek the quickening of the Holy Spirit in our own hearts, in our faith, in our prayer and testimony. It is most important also that we keep ourselves and all that we have under the protection of the blood. The enemy will use every possible means to silence our intercession and block our advancement against him. We must not only understand our enemy, our authority in Christ, and how to use our spiritual weapons, but also how to wear the armour God has provided for our protection. Thus equipped and protected, we need have no fear. But let us always remember that we of ourselves have no power and no authority outside of Christ. **L.M.**

Now thanks be unto God, which always causeth us to triumph in **Christ. II Cor. 2:14.**

Greater is he that is in you, than he that is in the world. **I John 4:4.**

Who prays
for the sinners?

For this is good and acceptable in the sight of God our Saviour; who will have all men to be saved, and to come unto the knowledge of the truth. I Tim. 2 : 3, 4.

The Lord . . . is longsuffering to us-ward, not willing that any should perish, but that all should come to repentance. II Peter 3 : 9.

It came as a great shock and challenge to me the other day while reading Christ's great intercessory prayer that He does not pray for sinners. He prays for His followers, disciples, and all who shall believe on His Name, but not for sinners. I did find that Jesus intercedes at the right hand of the Father, granting requests to His followers and offering forgiveness to the penitent sinner—but still does not pray for them.

This then is what challenged me—if Christ has left to His followers the work of praying for sinners, what kind of praying and how much praying am I doing for them? If it depends upon your praying and upon my praying for their salvation what chance do they have? There may be a lot of things many of us cannot do, but all can pray.

I also read that "no man cometh unto the Father except the Spirit draw him". Who is going to travail and prevail until the Spirit does draw sinful men unto the Saviour? There is an abundance of drawing power stored up at the throne of God but still we have to ask that it be released upon a specific individual. I am fearful lest we contract the disease of softness, and be too concerned about our night's sleep, our regular meals, freshly-pressed trousers and our un-calloused knees to ask, seek and knock until the heavens open and faith takes hold of God's promise and the Spirit draws sinful men unto the Saviour.

Praying in the will of God we get that for which we ask. Therefore, be specific and let God know what you desire, and then hold on fervently until the answer comes. If you are praying for the salvation of sinful men this is truly the will of

God and you can expect an answer of "Yes, I will save, for this I gave My life."

Try taking one soul or one family and really effectually press the Throne of Grace until assurance comes that you have been heard even though they may not appear in your church the next Sunday. "Faith is still the victory."

Some people say there is so much to pray for that they don't know where to begin. If this exists start with yourself and then the Spirit will breathe through you the things which are most urgently requiring an answer. Souls are lost and we will never be challenged to pray for them until, through the eye of faith, we see in them potential saints.

Will you rise up and put on the fighting garments of prayer? They are neither beautiful nor brilliant, but they are absolutely powerful in the tearing down of the strong-holds of Satan.

Christ prays not for the sinner; angels have not been given the privilege. It is given to you, who love the Christ, to pray for that lost soul. This, then, is the challenge—Will You Pray?
G. D. Watson.

> Enlarge thy heart,
> Let others too share of thy prayers.
> Pray not alone for those whom thou
> Dost love—pray "for them also"
> Who have never heard, that hearing,
> In the hearing of His Word shall it receive,
> And in the Lord, the Saviour of the world,
> Believe.

Mary Mozley

Pray for "all men". We usually pray more for **things** than we do for **men.** Our prayers should be thrown across their pathway as they rush in their downward course to a lost eternity.
E. M. Bounds.

When begging is right

Ask what I shall do for thee. II Kings 2:9.

Thou hast asked an hard thing: nevertheless . . . it shall be so. II Kings 2:10.

Griffith John, who spent years in China as a missionary, wrote:

"It is God's will that we should ask, and that blessings should be bestowed in answer to our asking. Such is the Divine will; such is the Divine order. There are blessings which cannot be bestowed except in response to the asking.

"'God's will,' it has been said by someone, 'will be done with our help or without it.' Is that true? Is it true in the physical realm? God has His will with regard to the harvest; but it will never be done without the help of the husbandman. God has His will with regard to the progress of the race in material prosperity; but it will never be done without the co-operation of man.

"And so it is in the spiritual realm. God has His will with regard to the evangelisation of the world, but the world will never be evangelised without the co-operation of the preacher and the teacher. 'It must be done by both; God never without me, and I never without God.' And hence the need of work and prayer; not work without prayer and not prayer without work.

"Some would have us look upon work as the one thing needful. The value of work is obvious to them, but they cannot see why prayer should be regarded as indispensable. But why should not man beg? Why should he not ask as well as work? Work and prayer are not mutually antagonistic. They go hand in hand, and both are necessary. Jesus was one with God, and yet He did beg. He begged for Himself, and He begged for His disciples. Paul lived in close fellowship with God, and yet he was ever begging—begging for himself, and

112

begging for his churches.

"Luther was a tremendous worker, and he was a man mighty in prayer. With what earnestness did George Muller work for the orphans of England! Yes, and with what earnestness did he beg for them! What could George Muller have accomplished without prayer? In fact, the man who lives near to God, and who is ever striving to serve God, cannot but beg—beg constantly, beg persistently. He has learnt by personal experience how much depends upon begging, how the most precious gifts of Heaven are at the disposal of the man who can beg aright, who can beg well.

"There is not a man among us who would not have been much richer in nobility of character and wealth of good deeds if he had learnt the art of begging of God more thoroughly.

" 'Looking back at the end,' says Andrew A. Bonar, 'I suspect there will be great grief of our sins of omission—omission to get from God what we might have got by praying.' Thus it is the will of God that we should ask, and that blessings should be bestowed in answer to our petitions."

If we find that individuals are employed to change the face of continents by exploration or personal effort, why may not individuals equally prevail where they, by prayer, lay hold of the arm of the Almighty? I believe that the day will declare that solitary individuals have, simply by their prayers, prevailed to introduce the Gospel into vast populous dominions. The ancient Jewish Church was not directly evangelistic, yet, like David, who prepared the materials for the temple which another was to build, the Jewish Church provided an immense store of intercessions, which became available a thousand years afterwards. **Dr. Summerville.**

Fasting
with a purpose

In fastings often. II Cor. 11 : 27.

Four days ago I was fasting until this hour; and at the ninth hour I prayed in my house. Acts 10 : 30.

The demands of life upon our time are such that if we make way for the spiritual exercises there must be a fasting from something. The body demands time and attention; the soul with its claimant cry for mental and cultural development; the family with its obligations of love and society in which we live ever presenting a thousand needs any one of which could occupy a life-time of devotion. All clamour for our twenty-four hours.

"Fasting is abstaining from all that interferes with prayer," said Andrew Bonar. A book-lover, he had to fast from some of his over-weaning love for reading to make time for cultivating his friendship with God.

Home-makers, mothers and wives, in order to pray have had to fast from pleasurable side-lines that other women could indulge in. Knitting, rug-making, cooking exotic dishes—these were laid aside for spiritual values.

Phillips Brooks says of fasting : "It is the voluntary disuse of anything innocent in itself, with a view to spiritual culture."

Andrew Murray defines prayer and fasting in these words : "Prayer is reaching out after the unseen; fasting, letting go of all that is seen and temporal. Fasting helps express, deepens, confirms the resolution that we are ready to sacrifice anything, even ourselves, to attain what we seek for the kingdom of God."

Those who have full daily programmes, sometimes fast from late-night social pleasures with family and friends and retire to quiet and rest that they might rise at an early hour to pray. John Wesley would punctually leave company at 9 o'clock that he might recollect his thoughts before God before retiring, but at 4 o'clock in the morning he was up to get unmolested time for cultivating God.

Some have fasted from sleep to give a night now and again to a vigil of prayer for some cause or person. Some have fasted from a higher education as did Joseph Kemp when, a young minister in Edinburgh, he was located with Charlotte Chapel Baptist Church. Members were few, the church almost empty but Edinburgh offered educational advantages to the ambitious young minister. Prayer for revival, demanding every night prayer-meetings, would have to be laid aside if he indulged his legitimate desire for further education. Fasting from this, he engaged in travail until revival was born to Charlotte Chapel.

We associate fasting largely with fasting from food but this is only a small part of the idea of fasting. It is perhaps more in our minds because the desire for food is the most persistent, most regular and frequent. This being the most animal-like appetite, fasting now and again helps to "keep the body under". Doctors tell us how beneficial occasional fasts are for the physical well-being.

David Brainerd's diary reads this way for a Thursday : "Being sensible of the great want of divine influences and the outpouring of God's Spirit, I spent this day in fasting and prayer to seek so great a mercy for myself, my poor people in particular, and the Church of God in general. In the morning, I was very lifeless in prayer and could get scarce any sense of God. Near noon, I enjoyed some sweet freedom to pray that the will of God might in every respect become mine, and I am persuaded it was so at that time in some good degree."

David Livingstone had this practical bit of advice to give : "Fastings and vigils without a special object in view are time run to waste. They are made to minister to a sort of self-gratification, instead of being turned to good account. The forty days of Lent might be annually spent in visiting adjacent tribes, and bearing unavoidable hunger and thirst with a good grace."

Is not this the fast that I have chosen ? to loose the bands of wickedness, to undo the heavy burdens, and to let the oppressed go free, and that ye break every yoke ? **Isa. 58 : 6.**

Morning delinquency

One lamb thou shalt offer in the morning. Exod. 29 : 39.

Joshua rose early in the morning. Josh. 3 : 1, 6 : 12, 7 : 16, 8 : 10.

Job rose up early in the morning and offered burnt offerings. Job. 1 : 5.

The Bible has mornings! Today we stay up so late that the blush of dawn is unheralded by man. Only the birds and wild life greet the dawn, except it be for shift workers or the milkman, and perhaps a few veterans, square enough to observe the morning watch!

God loved to deal with His people in the morning. In Revelation, He is called the morning star of the early dawn. In the Old Testament He revealed Himself to His servants very often in the morning. Abraham got up early to stand before the Lord. Jacob rose up early in the morning to make an altar. Moses rose up early in the morning, at God's command, to meet with Pharaoh.

In the morning, the Lord looked down from Heaven and saw the Egyptians pursuing His people and He did something about it in the morning—"He troubled the host of the Egyptians". He sent bread from Heaven in the morning hours for the vast host of Israel. No sacrifice kept over night was good enough for the morning. It must be fresh. A lamb was offered each morning and night. Incense was offered morning and night. Free offerings were offered in the morning.

A famous evangelist made a survey of two leading theological schools in the United States. Five hundred students were questioned and 93% of them said they had no devotional life. We wonder what would be the statistics if the majority of Christians were questioned!

Get up, get up for Jesus,

The power of sloth is strong
And if you want to get up,
    You must not lie too long;
You may be tired with toiling,
    Yet love will stand the test.
To all who come, though weary,
    Christ gives a better rest.

Unknown

In fellowship with Him I must strike the key-note of the day.
I almost think sometimes that the modern day has no morning,
and that the lack of a true morning is the great lack of
modern Christianity. The habit of giving the best of the life to
vigorous outwardness of Christian service, and leaving the
worst of it for prayer, so praying when both soul and body
are dropping asleep, is that which makes our Christianity so
shallow. Even some revivalists have almost forgotten the
meaning of morning. When, after the hot-house forcing
processes of a late meeting, followed by a short night, you
start up half awake, snatch something from the table, and
run to catch the train—that interval of hurry is not what the
Psalmist means by morning! He means morning with dew in it
—morning when, instead of being dull as a clod, you are
keen as a star, morning when you are at your freshest and
best, the sweet morning moments, so clear, so calm, so
bright, that come before you are tired, when life as yet has no
fever in it, no hurry and no delirium; when, while you are
meeting at the Throne of Grace, you are all there.

If you would have sudden kindlings of celestial lightning
within you, and keen strings of concentrated conviction; if you
would have pronounced theology, if you would know the bloom
and delicacy of grace, mind the morning. **Charles Stanford, D.D.**

The difference between rising at five and seven o'clock in the
morning, for the space of forty years, supposing a man to go
to bed at the same hour at night, is nearly equivalent to the
addition of ten years to a man's life. **Doddridge.**

One hour gained by rising early, is worth one month in a year.

Priority to the King's word

I have not spoken in secret, in a dark place of the earth . . . I the Lord speak righteousness, I declare things that are right. Isa. 45 : 19.

My son, if thou wilt receive my words, and hide my commandments with thee . . . then shalt thou understand the fear of the Lord and find the knowledge of God. For the Lord giveth wisdom : out of his mouth cometh knowledge and understanding. Pro. 2 : 1, 5, 6.

George Muller relates his mistake as a young Christian, in giving priority to the counsel of others rather than to the King.

"I fell into the snare, into which so many young believers fall, the reading of religious books in preference to the Scriptures. I could no longer read French and German novels, as I had formerly done, to feed my carnal mind; but still I did not put into the room of those books the best of all books. I read tracts, missionary papers, sermons and biographies of godly persons. The last kind of books I found more profitable than others, and had they been well selected, or had I not read too much of such writings, or had any of them tended particularly to endear the Scriptures to me, they might have done me much good.

"I never had been at any time in my life in the habit of reading the Holy Scriptures. When under fifteen years of age, I occasionally read a little of them at shool; afterwards God's precious Book was entirely laid aside, so that I never read one single chapter of it, as far as I remember, till it pleased God to begin a work of grace in my heart.

"Now the Scriptural way of reasoning would have been : God Himself has condescended to become an Author, and I am ignorant about that precious Book, which His Holy Spirit has caused to be written through the instrumentality of His servants, and it contains that which I ought to know, and the knowledge of which will lead me to true happiness. Therefore I ought to read again and again this most precious book, this book of books, most earnestly, most prayerfully, and with much meditation; and in this practice I ought to continue all the days of my life . . . But instead of acting thus, and being led by my ignorance of the Word of God to study it more, my difficulty in understanding it, and the little enjoyment I had in it, made me careless of reading it (for much prayerful reading of the Word, gives not merely more knowledge, but increases the delight we have in reading it).

"Thus, like many believers, I practically preferred, for the first four years of my divine life, the works of uninspired men to the oracles of the living God. The consequence was, that I remained a babe, both in knowledge and grace. In knowledge I say; for all **true** knowledge must be derived, by the Spirit, from the Word. And as I neglected the Word, I was for nearly four years so ignorant, that I did not **clearly** know even the **fundamental** points of our holy faith.

"This lack of knowledge most sadly kept me back from walking steadily in the ways of God. For it is the truth that makes us free (John 8 : 31, 32), by delivering us from the slavery of the lusts of the flesh, the lusts of the eyes, and the pride of life. The Word proves it. The experience of the saints proves it; and also my own experience most decidedly proves it. For when it pleased the Lord to bring me really to the Scriptures, my life and walk became very different. And though even since that I have very much fallen short of what I might have been and ought to be, yet, by the grace of God, I have been enabled to live much nearer to Him than before.

"If any believers read this, who practically prefer other books to the Holy Scriptures, and who enjoy the writings of men much more than the Word of God, may they be warned by my loss."

The words of the Lord are pure words. **Psa. 12 : 6.**
The word of the Lord is tried. **Psa. 18 : 30.**

A Godly man
is a praying man

**For this shall every one that is godly pray unto thee.
Psa. 32 : 6.**

**I will therefore that men pray every where, lifting up holy
hands. I Tim. 2 : 8.**

It is prayer-force which makes saints. Holy characters are
formed by the power of real praying. The more of true saints,
the more of praying; the more of praying, the more of true
saints.

More time and early hours for prayer would act like magic
to revive and invigorate many a decayed spiritual life. More
time and early hours for prayer would be manifest in holy
living. A holy life would not be so rare or so difficult a thing,
if our devotions were not so short and hurried . . .

The holier a man is the more does he estimate prayer; the
clearer does he see that God gives Himself to the praying
ones, and that the measure of God's revelation to the soul is
the measure of the soul's longing, importunate prayer for God.

Salvation never finds its way to a prayerless heart. The
Holy Spirit never abides in a prayerless spirit. Preaching
never edifies a prayerless soul. **E. M. Bounds.**

A godly man is a praying man. As soon as grace is poured
in, prayer is poured out. Prayer is the soul's traffic with
Heaven; God comes down to us by His Spirit, and we go up
to Him by prayer. **T. Watson.**

William Burns, a missionary in China and for a time a
colleague of Hudson Taylor in his youthful days, experienced
great revival blessing in the North of Scotland. The secret of
his power was prayer—much prayer—intercessory prayer. He
prayed hours daily. On one occasion when his mother entered
his bedroom to call him for breakfast, she found him lying on

the floor where he had been all night pleading with God. "Mother," he said, "God has given me Scotland today!"

G. H. Lang heard Fred Arnot, missionary explorer to Africa tell "that he had lodged with the elderly folk who, long years before, had entertained Burns at the time of the outpouring of the Spirit at Kilsyth. The day before, Saturday, Burns did not come down to breakfast, but they did not disturb him, supposing that he was taking extra rest. Nor did he appear at the midday meal, but still they left him undisturbed. But when again at tea, there was no sign of their guest they felt it a duty to ascertain whether he was yet alive and well. Opening the door gently, it was to see the preacher stretched on the floor in prayer. The next day the heavenly floods swept the congregation with a deluge of saving grace." *

Hudson Taylor relates how when they evangelised China together, one would speak for twenty minutes while the other prayed and then the rôles would be reversed. Burns' views influenced Hudson Taylor in the formation of the C.I.M.

The following are excerpts from a sermon preached by William Burns :

"No-one who is a stranger to closet religion can be a Christian. No-one who is without communion with the living God can be a Christian. No man who is not forsaking every known sin can be a Christian. No man who refuses to discover to be sin, that which God's Spirit in His Word has discovered to be Christ-dishonouring, can be a Christian. No; sin cannot live in the chambers of God's people, it cannot be carried into the secret of His presence, it cannot be indulged in the holiest of all. Those who are holding their idols to their hearts, and setting up their sins as stumbling blocks before their eyes, are not Christians, but hollow professors and self-deceivers.

"Acquaintance with God is the end of the divine life. If any of you shrink from this, and draw back from His presence, you give proof that you know not Christ, nor His salvation. If you did, you would be found pressing forward to gaze on His holy perfections as so many chambers of safety for your souls."

*From the writings of G. H. Lang. By permission.

A sense of inadequacy induces prayer

And when they in their trouble did turn unto the Lord God of Israel, and sought him, he was found of them. II Chron. 15 : 4.

Their soul fainted in them. Then they cried unto the Lord in their trouble. Psa. 107 : 5, 6.

We do not pray at all until we are at our wits' end. "Their soul fainted in them. **Then** they cried unto the Lord in their trouble" (Psa. 107 : 6, 13, 19, 28). When a man is at his wits' end it is not a cowardly thing to pray, it is the only way he can get in touch with Reality. "O that I knew where I could get into touch with the Reality that explains things!" There is only one way, and that is the way of prayer. (See I John 5 : 14, 15). **Oswald Chambers.**

It is when we realise our need that we pray and prevail. So long as we think we can manage without God we do not trouble to cry unto Him. That is why the answer is sometimes delayed. The trial gathers intensity as the crisis deepens. The need gets desperate, and prayer becomes fervent. All other help is cut off, and the soul is flung back upon God. Our moment of extremity becomes God's opportunity, and He appears glorious in holiness, doing wonders. Whitefield said in one crisis of his life : "I have thrown myself blindfold into His almighty arms." Though our resources seem ridiculously inadequate they must not be withheld. God often works by what we have. The widow had to use her little oil and meal, and the lad had to give up his five barley cakes and two small fishes. Weapons that are useless in our hands become mighty in His. Methods are nothing apart from inspiration, and the most faulty tools are better with Him than the most approved without Him.* **Samuel Chadwick.**

One of Satan's master-devices is to arrest our prayers. And he delights to do this by making us satisfied with earthly things. A serene and settled life discounts the necessity of prayer. It is when we are driven hither and thither that we are compelled to pray. Changes extort supplication. Had some of us always been wholly at ease and quiet, we would have ceased to pray, but God averted that catastrophe by piercing our poor life with changes. In the day the heat consumed us, and in the night the cold froze us, till we had to cry day and night, "Lord, help me!" Changes are the price we pay for proficiency in prayer. **Dinsdale Young.**

The petty trials this life begets
   My weary soul oppressed.
My strength had waned, and courage failed,
   My spirit sore distressed.
'Twas then in desperate urgency
   I sought strength—not my own,
And thought to hurl a mighty plea
   Afar to God's bright throne.

I raised my eyes and sought for words;
   "Dear Father . . .," then I cried.
But ere another word was formed
   I sensed Him at my side.
No lightning rent the midnight sky,
   Nor did the thunder roll,
And yet great waves of glory
   Engulfed my trembling soul.

I felt His arm—He drew me close.
   His voice was as a song,
"I know thy need, but tell Me, child,
   Why didst thou wait so long?"
Now when I need His special help
   To stem the swelling tide,
No longer beams my frantic cry—
   I know He's at my side!

John W. Little

❋From The Path of Prayer by Samuel Chadwick. (London: Hodder & Stoughton).
Copyright 1931 by Samuel Chadwick. Copyright 1956 Hodder & Stoughton Limited.

He pleads for us

We have an advocate with the Father, Jesus Christ, the righteous. I John 2:1.

He ever liveth to make intercession for them. Heb. 7:25.

O blessed feet of Jesus! Weary with seeking me,
Stand at God's bar of judgment and intercede for
me.

O Knees which bent in anguish in dark
Gethsemane,
Kneel at the Throne of Glory and intercede for me.

O Hands that were extended upon the awful tree,
Hold up those precious nail-prints and intercede
for me.

O Side from whence the spear-point brought blood
and water free,
For healing and for cleansing, still intercede for me.

Selected

We have, at this present moment, an Advocate actually remembering us in His thoughts, and presenting us to His Father. Without any faintness in the degrees of His intercession, without any interruption in time; He never ceases the exercise of this office.

Christ is an Intercessor for us in the whole course of our pilgrimage, all the time that we have any need of Him. His voice is the same still: "I will that they behold my glory which Thou hast given me", till they are wafted from hence to a full vision of it. This is the true end of His heavenly life, and His living for ever there: "Seeing He ever liveth to make intercession for them" (Heb. 6:25).

His advocacy is like His life, without end : as He died once, to merit our redemption, so He lives always, to make application of redemption. He would not answer the end of His life, if He did not exercise the office of His priesthood. It would not be a love like that of a God, if He did not bear His people continually upon His heart. He was the Author of our faith, by enduring the cross; and the Finisher of our faith, by "sitting down at the right hand of God" (Heb. 12 : 2). He will be exercised in it as long as there is any faith to be finished and completed in the world. His oblation was a transient act, but His appearance in Heaven for us is a permanent act and continues for ever . . .

The high priest entered into the holy of holies but once a year, but this High Priest sits forever in the court in a perpetual exercise of His function, both as a priest and a sacrifice. And since His own sacrifice for sins offered on earth was sufficient, He hath nothing to do perpetually in Heaven, but to sprinkle the blood of that sacrifice upon the mercy-seat. He is never out of the presence of God, and the infiniteness of His compassions may hinder us from imagining a silence in Him, when any accusations are brought in against us. The accusations might succeed well, were He out of the way; but being always present, He is always active in His solicitations. No clamour can come against us, but He hears it, as being on the right hand of His Father, and appears as our Attorney there in the Presence of God, to answer it, as the high priest appeared in the holy of holies for all the people . . .

As when He was on earth, never man spake as He spake; so now He is in Heaven, never did man or angel plead as He pleads. "If whatsoever we ask in His name", we shall receive (John 16 : 23), surely whatsoever He asks in His own name, will not be refused. **Stephen Charnock.**

If I could hear Christ praying for me in the next room, I would not fear a million enemies. Yet distance makes no difference. He is praying for me. **Robert Murray McCheyne.**

Christ . . . is even at the right hand of God, who also maketh intercession for us. **Rom. 8 : 34.**

For Christ is not entered into the holy places made with hands, which are the figures of the true; but into heaven itself, now to appear in the presence of God for us. **Heb. 9 : 24.**

Prayers bring in
his kingdom

And when he had taken the book, the four beasts and four and twenty elders fell down before the Lamb, having everyone of them harps, and golden vials full of odours, which are the prayers of the saints. Rev. 5:8.

And the smoke of the incense, which came with the prayers of the saints, ascended up before God out of the angel's hand. Rev. 8:4.

It is fitting in this last reading to consider what important place the prayers of all ages will have in Christ's final triumph. The fifth chapter of Revelation is majestic in its portrayal of the Lamb's exaltation which would be incomplete without the sweet odours of the prayers of the saints.

Let us view the scene as pictured by W. R. Newell in his commentary on Revelation: Why are harps and bowls full of incense which are the prayers of the saints connected with the Lamb's taking the book of the inheritance? Did the prayers of the saints bring about this scene? Would our Lord have commanded His disciples to pray "Thy Kingdom come, Thy will be done, as in heaven, so on earth", if prayers of the saints were not a vital factor in bringing about this glorious result? Follow through the book of Revelation whatever is said about the prayers of the saints. Some day it will be found that every soul that has been saved, every blessing any saint has received, every thwarting of Satan, every victory for God, as well as this final consummation of our Lord's taking over the book of the kingdom—all have been brought about through the saints' prayers, inspired of God, as essential elements in His great, all-comprehensive purpose.

This angel of Rev. 8:3 is publicly to bring before all Heaven three things:
1. That the prayers of all the saints are ever had in memory before God: a most blessed and solemn truth! No saint's prayer is forgotten, but has its effect in due season, in

bringing in the Kingdom, that is, our Lord's return!

2. That the incense (ever in Scripture setting forth the power of Christ's atonement **acting upon God**) the incense, I say, representing our Lord's person and work at Calvary, added in due time to the prayers of all the saints, makes them instantly effectual before God.

3. That the prayers of all the saints, in the power of Christ's atonement, **is that which really brings about judgment.** It is the answer at last to "Thy Kingdom come" which the saints of all ages have prayed. No other answer could be given, inasmuch as earth has rejected the rightful King!

It is of the utmost importance that we understand Revelation 8:3-5. This incense is "given" to this angel. (Christ would have needed none!) And it is God's hour to begin **from** Heaven that direct Heavenly intervention which will be the answer to the saints' prayers. Enoch prophesied of it (Jude 14, 15). Jacob waited for it (Gen. 49:18). All the prophets spake of it. Now, in Revelation 8:3-5—inasmuch as its hour has begun to be, what caused it must be openly brought in and shown upon "the golden altar which was before the throne" (of God).

Let my prayer be set forth before thee as incense. **Psa. 141:2.**

What a glorious privilege it is to feel we have a part in the greatest of all happenings—the bringing in of Christ's Kingdom. Never let us allow the enemy to deceive us by the lie that any prayer is ordinary and does not count or the burden we carry is some isolated problem of our own. What a dignity and honour it will add to our praying when we realise that it is immortal in its endurance and without limit as to its pervasive sweet savour.